English Syntax

English Syntax

A Guide
To The Grammar
Of Successful Writers

by Dick Heaberlin

Writing Style 1

Orange House Book

San Marcos, Texas

For Additional Information Visit the Author's Website at
dickheaberlinwrites.com

ISBN 978-0-9794964-1-7

Library of Congress Control Number
Library of Congress Subject Heading:

About This Book

I studied grammar at North Texas State with Mary Whitton, one of the authors of the Harbrace Handbook and later with Archibald A. Hill at the University of Texas. I loved the subject, and I enjoyed teaching it to my seventh grade language arts class at Dickinson Junior high in 1959. I was remarkably successful in teaching those seventh graders the basic structure of English sentences. I used a combination of the activities I now use in my guides to writing style. My students wrote sentences according to patterns, and they analyzed sentences to see how they were formed. I have continued those activities in the forty-eight years I have been teaching since then.

The basic idea is that I never expected my students to know the structure until I taught it. Then I expected them to know it and build on it to form or analyze increasingly complex sentences. I know that when writers know about English syntax and know about what structures can be used to accomplish a particular task, they write better and more confidently. Thus, they willingly write more.

For years I taught English Syntax and composition classes without the aid of my guidebooks, and I was successful, but since I have written them and have been using them, I find it easier to be successful. Students who are ill and get behind on their work particularly benefit. Some have even used the book without classroom instruction and have successfully completed the course. Several of my former students have reported to me that they have used some of the exercises from the guides in their own writing classes.

It is not my goal to teach every structure of English. It is not a comprehensive or scientific grammar that I teach but a pedagogic grammar, one designed to describe structures most useful for writers.

Contents

Lesson 1

Subject and Verb

Sentences are composed of subjects and verbs. In the sentence "Bob runs," **Bob** is the subject. The most common subject of a sentence is a noun, and the most common type of noun is one which refers to a human, such as *Bob, the boy, a teacher, some clowns*. The words *the, a, an,* and *some* are grammatical structure words called articles or determiners. They indicate that a noun follows.

The verb in the sentence "Bob runs," is *runs*. The verb in this sentence answers the question, "What does Bob do?" The answer is that he runs. The subject answers the question *who* before the verb. Who runs? *Bob* runs.

Exercise 1

In the following sentences, underline a noun once. Underline the verb twice and put a broken single line under any determiner. The answers to all exercises are in Appendix 1.

Example: The man cried.

1. Grover   moaned.

2. The   man   groans.

3. Some   pirates   whistle.

4. Susan   dances.

5. A   child   coughed.

6. Max   quit.

Verb Phrases. Verbs frequently appear in the single word forms. They have no ending or the ending *-s* or *-ed* as shown by *whistle* (no ending), *groans*, and *groaned*. These endings will help you recognize the verb. They also give you general information about the time of the action. The ending *-ing* in "Bob is eating" helps tell us that Bob is eating right now, that the eating is in progress. Notice that the *is* form of the auxiliary verb *be* precedes the main verb and the *-ing* follows and is attached to the main verb. The forms of the verb *be* are *be, is, am, are, was, were, been,* and *being* Both the auxiliary verb and the *-ing* ending are necessary to convey this idea of the action being in progress.

Exercise 2

Follow the directions for Exercise 1 in marking the following sentences. Also underline your auxiliary verb with two lines.

Example: The coward is whining.

1. Manuel   is   singing.

2. Some   babysitters   cry.

3. The   dancer   slipped.

4. The   actresses   are   perspiring.

5. The   roof   was   leaking.

6. The   babies   were   smiling.

Perfect Tenses of Verbs. In the sentence "Bob has eaten," we see another ending. This ending is referred to as the past-participle ending and this ending attached to the verb combines with a form of the verb *have* before the verb to convey the idea that the action is complete. The other forms of the verb *have* are *has* and *had*.

```
I have eaten.

He has eaten.

He had eaten.
```

The verb *eat* like a few other verbs in English has five forms.

```
The students eat  .            (No ending)

The student eats.              (Present tense)

The student is eating.         (Present progressive tense)

The student ate.               (Past tense)

The student has eaten.         (Present Perfect tense)
```

Most verbs have only four forms.

```
The students cook  __ .        (No ending, present tense)

The student cooks.

The students cooked.           (Past tense)

The students had cooked.       (Past Perfect tense)
```

Notice that *-ed* is the most common past participle ending. It is identical to the past ending of regular verbs.

Some verbs have only three forms. They usually end in *t* or *d*. A good example is *cut*. The present tense, past tense, and past participle are all *cut*.

```
I usually cut my hair.        (Present tense)

I cut my hair yesterday.      (Past tense)

I have cut my hair recently.  (Present Perfect tense)
```

Exercise 3

Mark the following sentences as you did in Exercise 2.

```
Example:  Bob has whimpered.
```

1. The   man   has   stuttered.

2. Gina   lies.

3. Marvin   has   whimpered.

4. The   bandits   have   escaped.

5. The   players   are   coming.

6. The   children   have   finished.

Modal Auxiliary Verbs. Another type of structure word used with the verb to tell us the time of the verb is the modal auxiliary. The modals are *will, shall, can, may, must, would, should, could, might.* All of these words when used with one main verb tell us the action will take place in the future. All but *will* and *shall* also give other information unrelated to time. These may combine with the other auxiliary verbs.

Exercise 4

Mark the following sentences as you did in Exercise 2.

1. The   man   will   paint.

2. Terry   should   stop.

3. Elizabeth   is   whistling.

4. A   paratrooper   may   jump.

5. Mr.   Jones   can   escape.

6. Harry   must   start

Lesson 2

Adverbials

There are several concepts conveyed by adverbials, words and phrases which modify a verb. One common adverbial is the adverb. Certain endings mark adverbs, -ly, -ways, -wards, and –wise. The most frequently used is –ly, usually for modifying the verb to tell how something is done. We consider other single words not marked with an ending adverbs because they can be compared.

Adverbs of Time. As you know, verbs are marked for time by their auxiliary words and their endings. More precise time can be conveyed with an adverb. An adverb of time is a modifier of the verb. Some examples of adverbs of time are *soon, now, yesterday, today, tomorrow, later*. The adverbs of time answer the question *when*.

Exercise 1

Underline subjects once and verbs twice. Underline adverbs with a wavy line and draw a line to the verb phrase.

    Example: Gilbert quit yesterday.

1. Bob   understands   now.

2. The   girl   is   leaving   tomorrow.

3. The   girl   will   leave   tomorrow.

4. The   girl   leaves   tomorrow.

5. The   child   cried   later.

6. Bill   ate   early.

7. The   boy   is   speaking   now.

Adverbs of Place, Direction. You have learned that adverbs of time answer the question *when* and modify the verb. The verb can also be modified by an adverb of place which answers the question *where* or *in what direction*: for example *here, there, away, above, out,* and *under*. The various auxiliary verbs introduced in earlier lessons may be used together.

Tom <u>may be leaving</u> **soon**.

Tom <u>should have walked</u> away.

Tom <u>could have been working</u> **alone**.

Tom <u>has been swimming</u> **already**.

Exercise 2

Underline the sentences as you have been.

Example: <u>The boy</u> <u>sat</u> **there yesterday**.

1. William   was   lying   here   then.

2. The   captain   may   move   away   soon.

3. Gabby   has   been   sitting   up.

4. The   child   will   fall   down   now.

Adverbs of Manner. Adverbs of manner answer the question *how* following the verb. Adverbs of manner are frequently marked by an **-ly** ending added to an adjective in form: e.g. **carefully, restively, cautiously**.

<u>How</u> did he enter?

<u>He</u> <u>entered</u> **cautiously**.

Exercise 3

Mark the structure of the following sentences as you have been in previous exercises.

1. The   unhappy   children   were   leaving   regretfully.

2. A   young   alligator   moved   lazily.

3. The   plumber   fixed   the   pipes   clumsily.

4. Bob   will   polish   the   floors   carefully.

5. Some   people   sing   marvelously.

Lesson 3

Sentence Patterns With and Without Direct Objects

$\underline{S}\ \underline{\underline{V}}_{\underline{T}}\ \underline{DO}$

The nouns used up to now in this book have referred to humans. Now we can direct our attention to other nouns that humans contact, things we see, touch, taste, smell, or hear. Nouns that refer to things we can contact with our senses are called concrete nouns: for example, a dog, Lassie, a chair, a flower, The White House, bacon, water, an arm. In our sentences we sometimes want to describe our contact with these items: for example, "The boy saw the chair. The boy hit the chair." The noun that precedes the verb is the *subject*. The noun that answers the question *whom* or *what* following the verb is called the *direct object* of the verb. A verb which has a direct object is called a *transitive verb*.

Exercise 1

Underline the sentences as you have been. In addition, write **S** above the subject, **V**t above transitive verb, and **DO** above the direct object.

$$ \qquad\qquad\qquad S \qquad V_T \qquad\qquad DO $$
Example: <u>Millie</u> <u>ate</u> the <u>dessert</u> <u>here</u> <u>yesterday</u>.

1. Malcolm   can   see   the   table   now.

2. The   dog   chased   the   cat   away.

3. The   children   were   teasing   the   horse.

4. Meg   liked   nutmeg.

5. The   workers   were   putting   the   hay   away.

6. The   cat   has   been   eating   the   plants.

7. Charlotte   may   have   been   wearing   the   dress   yesterday.

S V<u>I</u>

Verbs which do not have objects are called *intransitive verbs*. Some verbs never have an object and are always intransitive: e.g. *The dog growled.* Other verbs may have the object stated in one sentence—*Hazel ate the meal early*—and not stated in another—*Hazel ate early.* If the object is not stated, traditional grammarians consider it an intransitive verb.

Exercise 2

In the following sentences, underline and write above the words as you have in the previous exercises. Add **V_I** for *intransitive verb* to the markings you used in the last exercise.

1. The pirates carried the gold away.

2. The people spread out then.

3. The artist may be painting a masterpiece.

4. The crab grabbed a finger.

5. Bill has left.

6. Apples have a core.

Lesson 4

Adjectivals

Words which function as modifiers of nouns are called adjectivals. The most common type of adjectival is also an adjective in form. It has certain endings which mark it as an adjective: for example *-ful, -ive, -ate, -ish, -y, -ible, -able*; for example, *careful, impressive, fortunate, foolish, smoky, eligible, capable.* If a word does not have one of these endings, it still may be considered an adjective in form if it can be compared using the endings *-er, -est* or the structure words *more* and *most: brief, briefer, briefest; impressive, more impressive, most impressive.*

Exercise.

Mark the structure of the following sentences as you have been in previous exercises. In addition use a broken single line for the adjective and draw a line to the noun it modifies. Also draw a line from the adverb to the verb it modifies.

Example: The careful hunter may see the birds there.

1. A fortunate lady found some pretty rocks here yesterday.

2. The restive crowd was booing the lazy shortstop.

3. The pesky kid is crying now.

4. Some smart people eat green vegetables.

5. A swift runner has arrived early.

6. Some childish people destroyed the political poster.

Adjectivals may answer the question "which" or "what kind of" before the noun.

Which boy stole the pie? The *big* boy stole the pie.

Lesson 5

Negatives

There are several different ways that sentences can be made negative. The most common is to use *not*. *Not* is by some grammarians set off into a separate part of speech They consider it a modifier of the whole sentence and call it a *structural negative*. Other grammarians have considered it an adverbial because of its position alongside or within the verb phrase. We will consider it an adverb and draw a line to the verb to show its modification. Another adverbial which is negative is *never*. *None, no one, nobody,* and *nothing* function as nominals, and *no* functions as an adjectival.

I am not happy

I am not sleeping.

I have not eaten.

I never went.

I have no money.

I have none.

Exercise

1. I have not finished the work.

2. Nobody came early.

3. Nothing works now.

4. I will never hear the news.

5. No one has completed those difficult assignments yet.

Lesson 6

Patterns With Linking Verbs

S V$_L$ PN

Till now we have used two types of verbs, *intransitive* and *transitive*. There is one other type of verb, *the linking verb*. One type of linking verb can be followed by a noun: for example, "*The big boy **is** the **catcher**.*" In this sentence the noun following the linking verb is a type of subject complement. Other terms used for this noun are predicate noun, predicate nominal, and predicate nominative. There are only three verbs in American English that are regularly followed by a predicate noun: *be, become,* and *remain.* The S V$_T$ DO pattern looks much like the S V$_L$ PN pattern:

$$\underline{\overset{S}{\text{Bob}}} \; \underline{\overset{V_L}{\text{is}}} \; \underline{\overset{PN}{\text{the plumber.}}}$$

$$\underline{\overset{S}{\text{Bob}}} \; \underline{\overset{V_T}{\text{knows}}} \; \underline{\overset{D.O.}{\text{the plumber.}}}$$

Notice that in the first sentence the word *Bob* and *plumber* refer to the same human, but in the second sentence Bob and the plumber are not the same person.

Exercise 1

Mark the following sentences as you have been. Add V$_L$ for linking verb and PN for predicate noun to your marking system.

1. Tom   is   a   carpenter.

2. The   man   became   a   dentist.

3. Some   boys   may   leave   soon.

4. Harold   threw   the   ball   accurately.

5. Rover   may   be   a   mutt.

6. The   girl   remained   the   captain.

S V L PA

Another type of complement of the subject is an adjectival which follows a linking verb. Some additional linking verbs are *feel, seem, appear, look, get, grow, turn,* and *act*. The adjective following these and modifying the subject is called a *predicate adjective*.

$$\underset{\text{Tom}}{\underline{S}} \; \underset{\text{is}}{\underline{V_L}} \; \underset{\text{sick.}}{\overset{PA}{\dotuline{}}}$$

Sick describes Tom's condition. It tells how he is. Notice that both the predicate adjective and adverb of manner answer the question *how*, but the *how* means something slightly different. As an adverb of manner, it tells the way the verb is done. How does Alice sing? Alice sings beautifully. In the sentence *How is Bob? how* is not asking about the way Bob does something but is asking about his condition. Some of these verbs may function as transitive and intransitive verbs also.

I felt the chair.

Tom looked away.

I got a job.

Notice that *chair* and *I* do not refer to the same thing and that *away* does not tell how Tom looked but where.

Exercise 2

Mark the following sentences as you have been. Also, put PA above any predicate adjective. We will save the trouble of drawing a line from the PA to the subject because it always modifies the subject.

Example: Mabel is happy now.

1. Ellen   has   been   angry   today.

2. George   fought   furiously.

3. The girl had completed her lessons.

4. Bill feels sick.

5. Herbert is a boxer now.

6. The little girl sat down gracefully.

7. The best pies are hot.

8. The teacher looked excited.

9. Marvin became a coach.

10. The man hid the eggs carefully.

Lesson 7

Prepositional Phrases as Adverbials and Adjectivals

Most frequently the adverbials of time and place are not single-word adverbs but are prepositional phrases — word groups made of prepositions and their objects. The object is most frequently a noun in form. In the sentence

$$\overset{S}{\underline{Alice}} \ \overset{V_{I}}{\underline{went}} \ [to \ \underline{the} \ \overset{OP}{\underline{movie}}.]$$

to the movie is a prepositional phrase answering the question *where* following the verb, so it must be an adverbial of time. *To* is the preposition and *the movie* is the object of the preposition because it can answer the question *what* following *to*.

$$\overset{S}{\underline{Alice}} \ \overset{V_{I}}{\underline{went}} \ [to \ \textbf{what}]? \quad \textbf{The movie is the answer.}$$

Exercise 1

Mark the following sentences as usual. Bracket the prepositional phrases and write OP above the object of the preposition. Draw a line from the first bracket to the word modified.

Example: $\overset{S}{\underline{Elizabeth}} \ \overset{V_{I}}{\underline{arrived}} \ [on \ \overset{OP}{\underline{Monday}}] \ [in \ \overset{OP}{\underline{Boston}}.]$

1. Elizabeth is happy in Boston.

2. The designer ordered the drapes from Paris.

3. Bill is a soldier on Saturday.

4. Some campers should go up the mountain during the afternoon.

5. The cats ate the food on the porch.

6. The kids were scattering after the party.

7. Bob had become ill before the party.

8. The horse seemed slow on the steep trail.

Prepositional phrases may serve as adjectivals even though they are not adjectives in form. In the sentence

The house [on the corner] is white.

on the corner functions as a modifier of *house* by telling which house. Which house is white? *The house on the corner* is the answer. A prepositional phrase as an adjectival may be within another prepositional phrase:

The boy lives [in the house [on the corner.]]

On the corner functions as the modifier of *house* which is the object of the preposition *in*.

Exercise 2

Mark these sentences as usual. In addition, for prepositional phrases as adjectivals, draw a line from the bracket to the word that the prepositional phrase modifies.

Example: The cat [at the bait stand] hated shrimp.

1. The tiger in the cage roared.

2. The boy on the bike threw the paper toward the steps of the house.

3. The old trapper had appeared angry on the first day.

4. The fans came through the gates of the stadium early.

5. The man on the roof must be careful.

6. An old man shelled some peas on the back porch yesterday.

7. The garden behind the house was beautiful in the early morning.

8. The man at the gate took the tickets.

Lesson 8

Personal Pronouns

The words that function as subjects, direct objects, and objects of prepositions are not always nouns in form. Words that function as subjects or objects are called *nominals*. Nouns are nominals, but so are pronouns. One type of pronoun functioning as a *nominal* is called the *personal pronoun*. The personal pronouns used for the subject nominal are *I, you, he, she, we, they,* and *it.* The personal pronouns used for the object nominal are *me, you, him, her, them,* and *it.* All the pronouns but *it* refer to human nouns. We also have indefinite pronouns to refer to an unspecified human — *somebody, someone, anyone, anybody* — and to an unspecified non-human — *something.*

Exercise

Mark the following sentences as usual. Use one line to underline pronouns.

                         S   V_T DO

Example: He ate it.

1. Mr. Simpson sent someone to the phone.

2. They had piloted the old barge down the quiet river.

3. She raised it sleepily.

4. Bob knew her at school.

5. Something is upsetting him.

6. We went to it late.

7. He smelled them near the gate.

8. The book on the desk was covering it.

9. I went to her after the class.

Lesson 9

Demonstratives and Possessives
As Adjectivals and Nominals

Some pronouns refer to people and things. There are the demonstrative and possessive pronouns which are used to replace noun phrases.

Demonstratives

$$S \quad V_T \quad DO$$
I like these.

$$S \quad V_T \qquad DO$$
Bob wanted those.

$$\quad S \qquad V_L \quad PA$$
This looks good.

$$S \qquad V_T \quad DO$$
That does it.

Possessives

$$S \quad V_L \quad PA$$
Mine got old.

$$S \qquad V_T \qquad D.O.$$
We will take hers.

$$S \qquad V_I \qquad OP$$
We will go [in his].

The demonstrative and possessive words in these sentences all function as nominals, so it is correct to call them *pronouns*.

But when they serve as adjectivals, modifying the noun that follows, they are no longer pronouns in the strictest sense of the word. Some grammarians call them *determiners* since nouns invariably follow them.

$$S \quad V_L \quad PA$$
My dog got old.

$$S \qquad V_T \quad D.O$$
We will take her car

$$S \qquad V_I \qquad OP$$
We will go [in his boat].

The possessive adjectivals are *my, your, his, her, its, our,* and *their*. The possessive nominals are *mine, yours, his, hers, ours,* and *theirs*.

The demonstrative words are the same whether adjectival or nominal: *this, that, these, those*.

```
  S    VT          D.O.
  I   like  these  books.

    S    Vt            DO
  Bob  wanted  those  flowers.

   S      S      VL    PA
  This  answer  looks  good.

                  S    VT   DO
  That  final  step  does  it.
```

Exercise

Mark the following sentences.

1. My   shovel   is   sharp.

2. These   books   are   my   books.

3. Ours   runs   well.

4. Our   car   runs   well.

5. That   was   a   mistake.

6. The   dog   hid   its   bone.

7. Those   trees   are   growing   tall.

8. I   like   mine.

9. My   cat   may   be   sleeping.

Lesson 10

Passive Voice

S V_TP

We learned earlier that some verbs have a noun phrase that follows them which answers the question *what*. We called those verbs transitive and called the noun phrase the direct object. Sentences having transitive verbs and direct objects can be made passive.

```
        S    Vt            D.O.
The boy moved the chair.

        S    Vt         DO
The boy hit the chair.

        S    Vt         D.O
Millie ate the desert here yesterday.
```

These sentences can all be made passive.

```
         S        Vep              op
The chair was moved [by the boy].

         S        Vep              op
The chair was hit [by the boy].

         S        Vep                         op
The desert was eaten here yesterday [by Millie].
```

Notice that the object is moved forward and becomes the subject. The subject in the active voice sentence becomes the object of the preposition *by* and is moved to the end of the sentence. Notice also some form of the verb *be* must be added before the verb of action. In addition to the verb in the example, *was*, other forms that may be used are *be, am, is, are, were, been,* and *being*. Notice too that the main verb is in the past participle form, the same form which is used in the perfect tenses. Do not confuse the perfect and the passive. The main verb in the passive will be immediately preceded by a *be* verb.

Verbs in the perfect tenses can be made passive just as those can which are progressive and those with modals.

Bill has completed the assignment.

The assignment has been completed [by Bill].

Helen was washing the dog.

The dog was being washed [by Helen].

Notice that in all of these sentences we could leave out the prepositional phrase containing the preposition *by* and the former subject.

The chair was moved.

The chair was hit.

The desert was eaten here yesterday.

The cat was chased away.

The assignment has been completed.

The dog was being washed.

We will win the lottery.

The lottery will be won.

There is such a thing as an intransitive verb being made passive in English, but many people do not consider it good usage. It occurs when the intransitive verb has an adverbial prepositional phrase modifying it and the object of that preposition is moved forward to become the subject.

We talked [about the matter].

The matter was talked about [by us].

We will not consider this pattern further in this study. So you will never be right in your marking if you write VIP above the verb.

Exercise

Mark the following sentences as you have been.

Example: The cake was baked earlier [by Tim].

1. The car was repaired poorly.

2. Calvin was fired yesterday.

3. Bill treated her wound.

4. The tiger has been killed.

5. He has finished his work.

6. He was washing his clothes.

7. These may have been washed already.

8. The jewels were removed from the vault by an expert thief.

9. He has become a pilot.

10. He was being rewarded well for his work.

11. Walt has been the leader recently

Pattern With Indirect Object

S $\underline{V_T}$ IO DO

Some transitive verbs have in their meaning the idea of moving something.

```
S    VT         DO
I  sent  a  package.
```

If the writer or speaker chooses, he may indicate the receiver of the item. He may do this in either of two ways. He may employ a prepositional phrase as an adverbial of place following the direct object.

```
S    VT      D.O         OP
I  sent  a  package  [to Henry.]
```

Or he may simply place the name of the receiver before the direct object.

```
S    VT    IO      DO
I  sent  Henry  a  package.
```

This is a variation of the basic S V_T DO pattern and the receiver of the direct object is called the indirect object. Here are two more examples.

```
S    VT      IO          DO
I  gave  my friend  my old skates.

        S          VT       IO    DO
The quarterback  threw  the end  a pass.
```

Verbs that introduce this type of pattern are such words as *give, hand, toss, mail, send, throw,* and *write*.

Exercise

Mark these sentences.

1. Beth   mailed   her   boyfriend   some   cookies.

2. The   clerk   handed   me   my   groceries.

3. He gave a bicycle to me.

4. The boy sent his girlfriend some flowers.

5. The paperboy tossed me my paper.

6. I was reading the book carefully.

7. They had returned the answers to the teacher.

8. Pam mailed her friend a letter.

9. Bob may be angry now.

Pattern With Retained Object

S V_TP RO

Patterns with indirect object may be made passive.

$$\text{I gave Tom a toy.}$$
S V_T IO D.O

$$\text{Tom was given a toy [by me]}$$
S V_tp RO OP

Since there were two objects — *Tom* and *a toy*, only one could be moved forward to become the subject of the passive voice sentence. In the example above, I moved the indirect object to the front and retained the direct object at the rear of the sentence. I could refer to the direct object which is retained as the retained direct object, but it is conventional to call it just the retained object. Write RO above it when you mark sentences.

Notice that in the sentence *I gave Tom a toy*, I could have moved the indirect object over to the end of the sentence and made it the object of the preposition *to*

$$\text{I gave a toy [to Tom].}$$
S V_T D.O OP

It that case, if I make it passive, I will have no retained object.

$$\text{A toy was given [to Tom] [by me].}$$
S V_tp OP OP

Some people would only transform this sentence into the passive by doing it that way. Others think the following transformation is perfectly acceptable.

$$\text{I gave Tom a toy.}$$
S V_T IO DO

$$\text{A toy was given Tom [by me.]}$$
S V_tp RO OP

Exercise

Mark these sentences.

1. His employers sent him a check.

2. He was sent a check by his employers.

3. His employers sent a check to him.

4. A check was sent to him by his employers.

5. A check was sent him by his employers.

6. He was mailed a bomb.

7. I have been mistreated by my friends.

8. I may have been handed the receipt.

9. I was being given a haircut by Rudy.

10. Rudy was giving me a haircut.

Lesson 13

Pattern with Object Complement

S V$_T$ DO OC

S V$_T$ DO OC

There is another variation of the **S V$_T$ DO** pattern. Following certain verbs the direct object may be followed by a structure which complements it. Usually this structure is an adjectival or nominal.

$$S \qquad V_T \qquad DO \qquad OC$$
We elected Harry Truman President.

Harry Truman and *President* in this sentence both refer to the same person. Truman is the person. We affected him by causing him to be President. In another example, the direct object is complemented by an adjective.

We made our mother angry.

This complement of the direct object is logically called the *object complement*. Verbs which are frequently followed by the direct object with an object complement are *name, select, call, make, paint, choose, elect,* and *pick*.

Exercise

Mark the following sentences, and put OC above the object complement.

1. Bob called me a coward.

2. Harry painted his bike green.

3. Bill made his teacher happy.

4. Gabriel tossed me a hat.

5. I gave Harriet my lemon pie.

6. The senior class chose Mary favorite.

3. Our neighbor has been giving my mother some peaches.

7. Bill may be eating hamburgers in the cafeteria.

8. We selected Clara president of our class.

9. I called Bill a coward.

10. We named our baby Clem.

Lesson 14

Pattern with Retained Object Complement

$\underline{S} \ \underline{\underline{V}}_{TP} \ \underline{ROC}$

$\underline{S} \ \underline{\underline{V}}_{TP} \ \underline{ROC}$

When the pattern with the object complement is made passive, there is only one way to do it—the direct object moves forward and the object complement is retained at the rear, so we call it the retained object complement and mark it ROC. It will most commonly be either a nominal or adjectival.

Notice how our two example sentences from the previous lesson are made passive.

> S   V   D.O   O.C.
> We elected Harry Truman President.
>
> S V   D.O   OC
> We made our mother angry.
>
>   S   Vtp   R.O.C.
> Harry Truman was elected President [by us.]
>
>   S   Vtp   R.O.C.
> Our Mother was made angry [by us.]

Certain verbs will help you identify this pattern: *name, select, call, make, paint, choose, elect,* and *pick.*

Sometimes the structure word *as* may be added to the sentence to introduce the ROC. We won't bother to give a name to *as* when it introduces the ROC. We will just put SW above it to indicate that it is a structure word.

> S   Vtp   R.O.C
> He was selected chairman.
>
> S   Vtp   SW R.O.C
> He was selected as chairman.
>
> S   Vtp   SW R.O.C
> He was picked as captain.

Exercise

Mark these sentences.

                    S   Vtp   R.OC   OP

Example: The baby was named Gomer [by the father].

1.   He was elected cheerleader.

2.   He was given a reward.

3.   He has been picked as a tax examiner.

4.   He has given Susan an award.

5.   They are being elected now.

6.   We were selecting them yesterday.

7.   He made me mad.

8.   Max's car has been painted red.

9.   My car has been clean.

10. My car has been cleaned.

11. I always have considered him a fool.

12. He has always been considered foolish.

Practice 1

Exercise 1

Mark the sentences.

1. The ice storm had been predicted by some astute meteorologists.

2. The man on Channel 10 has been calling it a disaster.

3. Some people have fallen because of the slickness of the steps.

4. The steps below the library should be considered dangerous during an ice storm.

5. Bob Larsen may have been the best weather forecaster before his dismissal for drunkenness.

6. The station did pay him his severance pay willingly.

7 He should be angry about their treatment of him.

8. Before the show he had been drinking for several hours at a neighborhood bar with his friends.

9. He was selected as chief meteorologist in 1994.

10. He was given a plaque at the time in addition to a raise.

11. Bob may have been paid well for his success at weather prediction.

12. He might be getting a new job soon.

13. He could become a bartender.

Exercise 2

Mark the sentences.

1. I have been feeling sorry for Fred because of his illness.

2. I gave the candy to Fred in the cafeteria before lunch.

3. His illness should not be considered trivial.

4. Mine should not have been serious.

5. I have always been a healthy person.

6. He was not given the candy by a friend.

7. The candy was given him by an enemy.

8. I am the purveyor of the candy.

9. He does not consider me guilty.

10. I have been called a poisoner by his true friends.

11. I was just telling George the story about Fred today.

12. George is blaming me fro Fred's illness.

13. They consider my explanation inadequate.

Exercise 3

Mark the sentences.

1. He has been fishing in the lake since noon.

2. Some expert fishermen consider him a good fisherman.

3. He can cast a fly into a small spot excellently.

4. Fish have been caught by him in unlikely places.

5. The fish become wary in the late afternoon because of the long shadows.

6. I was given a fish yesterday by my neighbor.

7. I may remain happy with the fish.

8. I am not considered a good fisherman by Jimmy.

9. He could have been good at his job.

10. He is considered lucky by many of his friends.

11. He may have been cheating in the bass contest.

Lesson 15

Possessives

Nouns may have a possessive form: *Susan's* bike, *Susan's* husband, *Susan's* arm, Susan's walk. The possessive form, of course, is recognized by the apostrophe and **s** attached to it. These forms are called possessive, but several relationships are covered by this term, for it is obvious that Susan doesn't possess her husband, her arm, or her way of walking in the same way she does her bike. The noun in the possessive functions as an adjectival, for it can answer the question *which* before another noun.

Which bike did Bob ride?

He rode Susan's bike.

In addition to the noun form, there is a possessive pronoun that can replace both the possessive noun and the following noun.

I like Mary's horse.

I like hers.

I saw the boys' car.

I saw theirs.

The possessive pronouns are *mine, yours, his, hers, its,* and *theirs.* Also there is a possessive adjectival which replaces only the possessive noun and not the following noun.

I like Mary's horse.

I like her horse.

I saw the boy's car.

I like his car.

The possessive adjectivals are *my, your, his, her, its,* and *their.*

Exercise

Mark the following sentences as usual. Pay close attention to the functions of the possessive forms.

Example: Bob's dog likes mine.

1. My friend ate your apples during lunch at school.

2. Bob's horse bit him on his arm yesterday.

3. Your horse runs smoothly.

4. Mine is clumsy.

5. Your coach is your father.

6. The man in the car put his hand out.

Lesson 16

Clauses Modifying Verbs

The function of modifying a verb may be performed not just by adverbs and preposition phrases but also by complete clauses. As you know, adverbials modify verbs by providing information about many subjects, such as *in what place, in what direction, from what source, of what material, by what means, in what manner, for what reason, with what result, at what time, for what duration, with what frequency, with what intensity, with what effect, to what degree, under what conditions, with what person, by what person.* Some important semantic concepts are here. The concepts are not solely adverbial. Nor are all of these communicated by clauses. Notice, though, how similar the adverbial clause is to the adverbials we have already studied.

Bob arrived yesterday.

I had never seen him before.

I had never seen Bob [before his arrival.]

I had never seen Bob (before he arrived yesterday.)

Obviously, we can tell these structures apart by observing what, if anything, follows *before.* Is it a noun phrase or a complete pattern? The words that precede the complete pattern and introduce verb modifying clauses are called *subordinating conjunctions.* There are only a few of these which work like *before* and function as adverbs and prepositions also. Others are *since, once,* and *after.*

Partial List of One Kind of Subordinating Conjunction (Verb Modifying Clause Introducers, type 1, VMCI1)

since	in order that	provided that	when
so that	providing that	as if	unless
where	seeing that	as though	because
while	seeing as how	inasmuch as	before
as	now that	after	though
whereas	even though	even if	if
although			

Notice that *because of* is always a preposition and that *because* without *of* is always a VMCI$_1$.

Position of Verb-modifying Clauses

One thing which may help you identify verb-modifying clauses is their freedom of movement. They may appear at the first of a sentence, between subject and verb, or after the verbal.

$$\overset{VMCl}{(\text{If}} \ \overset{S}{\underline{\text{Wilt}}} \ \overset{V_I}{\underline{\text{comes}}},) \ \overset{S}{\underline{\text{I}}} \ \overset{V_C}{\underline{\text{leave}}}.$$

$$\overset{S}{\underline{\text{Ice cream}}}, \ \overset{VMCl}{(\text{when}} \ \overset{S}{\underline{\text{it}}} \ \overset{V_L}{\underline{\text{is}}} \ \overset{P.A.}{\underline{\text{well-prepared}}},) \ \overset{}{\underline{\text{is}}} \ \overset{P.A.}{\underline{\text{delicious}}}.$$

$$\overset{S}{\underline{\text{Ice cream}}} \ \overset{V_L}{\underline{\text{is}}} \ \overset{PA}{\underline{\text{delicious}}} \ \overset{}{(\text{when}} \ \overset{S}{\underline{\text{it}}} \ \overset{V_L}{\underline{\text{is}}} \ \overset{P.A.}{\underline{\text{well-prepared}}}).$$

Ellipsis in Adverbial Clauses

When the subject of the verb-modifying clause is the same as the subject of the main clause, portions of the verb-modifying clause may be omitted, usually the subject and auxiliary verb *be* or linking verb *be*.

$$\overset{VMCl}{(\text{While}} \ \overset{S}{\underline{\text{I}}} \ \overset{V_I}{\underline{\text{was running}}} \ [\text{in the race},) \ \overset{S}{\underline{\text{I}}} \ \overset{V_L}{\underline{\text{grew}}} \ \overset{PA}{\underline{\text{dizzy}}}.$$

$$\overset{VMCl}{(\text{While}} \{ \overset{S}{\underline{\text{I}}} \ \overset{?}{\underline{was}} \} \ \overset{V_I}{\underline{\text{running}}} \ [\text{in the race}]) \ \overset{S}{\underline{\text{I}}} \ \overset{V_L}{\underline{\text{grew}}} \ \overset{PA}{\underline{\text{weary}}}.$$

$$\overset{VMCl}{(\text{When}} \ \overset{S}{\underline{\text{I}}} \ \overset{V_L}{\underline{\text{am}}} \ \overset{PA}{\underline{\text{angry}}},) \ \overset{S}{\underline{\text{I}}} \ \overset{V_L}{\underline{\text{turn}}} \ \overset{PA}{\underline{\text{red}}}.$$

$$(\text{When} \{ \overset{S}{\underline{\text{I}}} \ \overset{V_L}{\underline{\text{am}}} \} \ \overset{PA}{\underline{\text{angry}}},) \ \overset{S}{\underline{\text{I}}} \ \overset{V_L}{\underline{\text{turn}}} \ \overset{PA}{\underline{\text{red}}}.$$

Exercise 1

Mark the following sentences. Write any words omitted into the sentence and mark them according to their function. See examples above.

1. When you get here, we will have a party.

2. I will eat where he ate.

3. Although he was disappointed by Marie, he still loves her.

4. Although angry with her, he will forgive her.

5 We quarreled. I haven't seen him since.

6. I will work if he brings the tools.

7. Now that he is rich, he will not know us.

8. After his fight with Marie, I left.

9 After he fought with Marie, I left.

Clauses Modifying Verbs, Type 2

In addition to the clauses introduced by the type one connectives, there are clauses modifying verbs which are introduced by such words as *wherever, no matter where, whenever, no matter when, however, no matter how, no matter why, whichever, no matter which, whoever, no matter who, no matter whose, whatever, no matter what.*

(No matter where you hide,) he will find you.

(Wherever you hide,) he will find you.

(No matter how fast you run,) he will catch you.

(However fast you run,) he will catch you.

(No matter whose house you buy,) you will still not be respected.

(No matter whom you marry,) your mother will not be happy.

(Whomever you marry,) your mother will cry.

Unlike the introducers in the previous lesson, these connectives have adverbial, adjectival, and nominal functions in the dependent clause.

Exercise 2

Mark the following sentences.

1. I will come to the party no matter what you say.

2. I will be happy no matter what present you give me.

3. However sick you are, you still must work.

4. Whenever he arrives, I can pick him up.

5. I finished my work in order that I might rest briefly.

6. Whatever you do while depressed, I will still care for you.

Lesson 17

Clauses and Infinitives of Reason

There are several conjunctions already introduced which convey information about motive or cause — *because, since, as, in order that, so that, so, that*. Notice the difference of meaning as they appear in similar sentences.

$$\overset{\text{VMCl}_1}{\text{(Because}} \ \overset{S}{\underline{\text{he}}} \ \overset{V_I}{\underline{\text{practiced}}}, \overset{S}{)} \ \overset{S}{\underline{\text{he}}} \ \overset{V_I}{\underline{\text{won}}}.$$

$$\overset{\text{VMCl}_1}{\text{(Since}} \ \overset{S}{\underline{\text{he}}} \ \overset{V_I}{\underline{\text{practiced}}}, \overset{S}{)} \ \overset{S}{\underline{\text{he}}} \ \overset{V_I}{\underline{\text{won}}}.$$

$$\overset{S}{\underline{\text{He}}} \ \overset{V_I}{\underline{\text{practiced}}} \ \overset{\text{VMCl}_1}{\text{(in order that}} \ \overset{S}{\underline{\text{he}}} \ \overset{V_I}{\underline{\text{might win}}}.)$$

$$\overset{S}{\underline{\text{He}}} \ \overset{V_I}{\underline{\text{practiced}}} \ \overset{\text{VMCl}_1}{\text{(so that}} \ \overset{S}{\underline{\text{he}}} \ \overset{V_I}{\underline{\text{might win}}}.)$$

$$\overset{S}{\underline{\text{He}}} \ \overset{V_I}{\underline{\text{practiced}}} \ \overset{\text{VMCl}_1}{\text{(that}} \ \overset{S}{\underline{\text{he}}} \ \overset{V_I}{\underline{\text{might win}}}.)$$

$$\overset{S}{\underline{\text{He}}} \ \overset{V_I}{\underline{\text{practiced}}} \ \overset{\text{VMCl}_1}{\text{(so}} \ \overset{S}{\underline{\text{he}}} \ \overset{V_I}{\underline{\text{could win}}}.)$$

Notice how similar in meaning the last four sentences are. About the only difference in the sentences is in the degree of formality of the connective. None of these are as likely to appear as is the infinitive phrase which conveys the same concept.

$$\overset{S}{\underline{\text{He}}} \ \overset{V_I}{\underline{\text{practiced}}} \ \ddagger \overset{\text{VMII}}{\text{in order}} \ \overset{\text{Isw}}{\text{to}} \ \overset{I_I}{\underline{\text{win}}}.\ddagger$$

Notice that when the subject of the infinitive and the subject of the main clause refer to the same thing, the subject of the infinitive and its structure word are omitted. Notice also that the adverbial infinitive phrase conveys the idea of reason. In other words, it answers the question *why*. It may be preceded by the structure words *in order*. I call these two words the verb modifying infinitive introducer or VMII. Notice that *in order that* introduces a complete clause but *in order* without the *that* will precede the structure words *for* or *to*, which introduce the subject of the infinitive or the infinitive. Like the verb-modifying clause to which it is similar, the infinitive phrase of reason may appear in several places in the sentence.

$$\overset{VMII}{} \quad \overset{I_b}{} \quad \overset{PA}{} \qquad \overset{V_I}{} \qquad \qquad \overset{OP}{}$$

Bob, ‡in order to be early,‡ arose [before sunrise.]

$$\overset{VMII}{} \quad \overset{ISW}{} \quad \overset{I_b}{} \qquad \overset{S}{} \quad \overset{V_I}{} \qquad \overset{OP}{}$$

‡In order to be early,‡ Bob arose [before sunrise.]

$$\overset{S}{} \quad \overset{V_I}{} \qquad \qquad \overset{OP}{} \qquad \overset{VMII}{} \quad \overset{ISW}{} \quad \overset{I_b}{} \quad \overset{PA}{}$$

Bob arose [before sunrise] ‡in order to be early.‡

The infinitive phrase may be in any of the basic patterns.

You may leave out the structure words *in order*, and you will still have an adverbial infinitive phrase.

$$\overset{ISW}{} \quad \overset{I_b}{} \quad \overset{PA}{} \qquad \overset{S}{} \quad \overset{V_I}{} \qquad \qquad \overset{OP}{}$$

‡to be early,‡ Bob arose [before sunrise.]

You may include the subject of infinitive and its structure word *for* if the subject of infinitive does not refer to the same thing as the subject of the main clause.

$$\overset{VMII}{} \quad \overset{SISW}{} \quad \overset{S}{} \quad \overset{ISW}{} \quad \overset{I_b}{} \quad \overset{PA}{} \qquad \overset{S}{} \quad \overset{V_t}{} \quad \overset{DO}{} \qquad \qquad \overset{OP}{}$$

‡In order for Bob to be early,‡ I woke him [before sunrise.]

Exercise

Mark the following sentences. Note the way I marked the infinitive phrases in the sentences above and employ the same marks in the exercises below. *SISW* stands for subject of infinitive structure word. It is always *for*. Remember that *for* also has two other functions as preposition and coordinating conjunction. *For is the only SISW. ISW* stands for infinitive structure word. It is always *to*. *To* is also a preposition. *To is the only ISW.*)

1. In order to be prepared for class, I reread my notes.

2. In order for him to be elected president, I must write this speech.

3. In order that I might be wealthy, I invested in a roulette wheel.

4. While I was studying in order to pass the test, I was not working.

5. To get the tickets, I stood in line for a long time.

6. After Bob worked so hard to pass the test, I talked to him about his fear of failure.

Lesson 18

Coordinating Conjunctions

There are just a few coordinating conjunctions. They make elements which are equal syntactically into compounds. The most frequently used are *or* and *and*. They are used most frequently because they compound elements within a clause, e. g. nominals, verbals, or adverbials.

I saw Bob and Fred.

My mother and father like me.

I washed and rinsed the dishes

I went [across the street] and [into the woods.]

I will see Bob or Fred.

And shows the logic of addition and *or* the logic of alternation.

I will see Bob or Fred.

S	Vt	CC	Vt	DO
Jason	loved	and	respected	Tiffany,

Dependent clauses can be coordinated.

We left (because Mary was sick) and (because Fred was drunk.)

Verbs can be coordinated.

S	V$_T$	V$_T$	CC	V$_T$	DO
Jason	loved,	respected,	and	admired	Tiffany.

And independent clauses and sentences can be coordinated.

I will not go [to the party], and I will not worry [about it].

I will wash the dishes, or I will clean the house.

I will not go [to the party]. And I will not worry [about it].

I will wash the dishes. Or I will clean the house.

Many of us were taught not to use these coordinating conjunctions to begin sentences, but in the most formal of prose most of our best writers use them. If you doubt it, just check the writers you like best.

In addition to those two coordinating conjunctions, there are others which can be used between independent clauses and sentences. Two of them connect the clauses by telling us that one of the clauses presents the reason and the other the effect. Notice the difference of order.

Napoleon's troops died [of starvation] [in Russia], for he had outrun his supply system.

She hit Tony, so he cried.

The two sentences show the difference in arrangement of the cause and effect , andthey suggest the difference in formality. Notice that if we exchange the connectives between the sentences, they do not seem quite right in degree of formality.

Napoleon had outrun his supply system, so his troops died of starvation in Russia
Tony cried, for she hit him.

In these examples, all of these clauses are independent and could be independent sentences.

She hit Tony. So he cried.
Napoleon's troops died of starvation in Russia. For he had outrun his supply lines .

The same causal relationship might be conveyed using a VMCI$_1$, thus giving you a dependent clause.

Tony cried (because she hit him.)
S   V$_T$ VMCI$_1$ S   V$_T$ D.O.

(Because she hit him,) Tony cried.
VMCI$_1$ S   V$_T$ DO   S   V$_I$

When you use the dependent clause, you may move it, thus being able to put either cause or result first.

Similar to *so* and *for* are *but* and *yet,* which are used to convey contrast or surprise.

Bob was late, but I did not mind.
S   V$_L$ PA   cc   S   V$_T$

We had little money, yet we survived.
S   V$_T$ DO   cc   S   V$_I$

Bob was late. But I did not mind.
S   V$_L$ PA   cc   S   V$_T$

We had little money. Yet we survived.
S   V$_T$ D.O.   cc   S   V$_I$

The same concept could have been conveyed by using the VMCI$_1$, *although.*

(Although Bob was late), I did not mind.
VMCI$_1$ S   V$_L$ PA   S   V$_T$

I did not mind (although Bob was late.)
S   V$_T$ VMCI$_1$ S   V$_L$ PA

But can also be used to connect elements within in a sentence. Then, it is usually a rather complicated way of conveying addition. Notice the similarity in these sentences.

I saw Bob and Susan.
I saw not only Bob but also Susan.

And and *or/nor* are always coordinating conjunctions. *Yet, but, so,* and *for* may have other functions.

I have not finished yet.
S   V$_T$

I went [for milk].
S   V$_I$ OP

I waited (so that he could go [with me]).
S   V$_T$ VMCI$_1$ S   V$_I$ OP

Exercise

Mark the following sentences.

1. Bob ate wisely, but he gained weight.

2. Bob and Ted did the work without other help.

3. He was fired, for he stole some things from his company.

4. He went to the grocery store for milk.

5. In order for him to be elected without a runoff, he must get a large majority of the urban vote.

6. I quit, so I am poor.

7. I quit so I could have more free time.

8. He was fired because he stole from his company and because he was insubordinate.

9 I talked to Hal and Tim about their opportunities for promotion.

Lesson 19

Independent Clauses Introduced By Conjunctive Adverbials

There are some words in English that are somewhat like mules, hybrids. The words we call *conjunctive adverbs* are like this, and you can tell by the name what kind of hybrids they are. They are telling about the logical relationship of one phrase to another, so they are conjunctive. But unlike conjunctions, they do not have to stay at the first of the phrase they introduce. Instead, like adverbs, they may move around. But some do have certain places they are more likely to be found. Notice how they are different from the coordinating and subordinating conjunctions.

The word *although* is always a subordinating conjunction, but *though* can be either a subordinating conjunction or a conjunctive adverb.

Here is a list of conjunctive adverbs, extensive but not exhaustive.

once, now, then, still, yesterday, later, afterwards, soon, later, earlier, henceforth, thereafter, hereafter, meantime, meanwhile, so far, concurrently, often, occasionally, infrequently, sometimes, again, once, ahead, overhead, therefore, thus, hence, consequently, however, nevertheless, still, instead, nonetheless, moreover, also, in addition, next, too, besides, accordingly, fittingly

There are prepositional phrases that function much like conjunctive adverbs.

```
 S   Vt                    OP              CA    S    VI              OP
 I  ran [for three touchdowns].  Moreover, I passed [ for two].
 S   VI                    OP          CA         S    Vt
 I  ran [for three touchdowns].  [In addition], I passed [for
 OP
two.]
```

Exercise

Mark the following sentences.

1. Bob complained regularly, but he would not work.

2. Although Susan works hard, she makes little money.

3. I lost my job. However, Bob was hired.

4. I lost my job. Bob was hired, though.

5. I lost my job. In contrast, Bob was hired.

6. I lost my wallet; consequently, I have no money.++

Practice 2

Exercise 1

Mark the sentences.

1. The anxious parents had been observing the children attentively.

2. Some people might consider them overprotective.

3. However, they should give the children their full attention.

4. They probably have been parents for years, and they may be aware of some dangers.

5. Bears have been seen nearby, and they are considered dangerous sometimes.

6. Otherwise, parents have been worrying without proper cause.

7. We were sent letters by the park service, but I remain confident of our safety.

8. Dogs and cats are being kept inside by some pet owners.

9. Dogs and bears do not become friends easily, so our dogs must be protected.

10 The neighborhood dog is called Leo or Rocky Road, for he has two owners.

11. We called him Ugly Puppy at first.

12. The house should be repainted before your party.

13. They might have been lying about the bears. Exercise 2

Exercise 2

Mark the sentences.

1. Some people are unhappy when they are given Romaine lettuce.

2. Although I have been reading a novel, I have not finished it yet.

3. Bill will be returning soon from his vacation even though he has not been missed.

4. Because of his laziness, we do not complete our work promptly.

5. Because he is exceedingly lazy, we are usually quite late with our assignments.

6. Our boss gave him a warning about his work habits before he left for his vacation.

7. Btefore his return we should plan a practical joke so that he will know about our affection for him.

8. If you return late, Tom may not be here when you arrive.

9. Despite your anger, your mother probably loves you.

10. In case of fire, you should evacuate the building even if you consider yourself safe.

Exercise 3

Mark the sentences.

1. Jim has been sending Milly messages about his concern for her welfare.

2. When she gets the messages from him, she feels happy, but no message is sent to him in return, for she is shy.

3. In order for him to be her beau, he must be encouraged because he is considered shy, too.

4. Because of her interest in him, she talks to her friend to get advice.

5. Her friend is a woman with impeccable credentials in matters of love since she has had four husbands.

6. While talking to her friend, she discovers the truth about her affection for Jim.

7. Therefore, she chooses him as her date for the first dance of the season.

8. She has never attended a dance before this, yet she has seen them and has heard about them from her friend.

9. He might be considered a poor catch by many people, but he is considered wonderful by Milly.

10. For her to be truly happy, she must wear a beautiful gown to the dance.

Exercise 4

Mark the sentences.

1.   The tree on the corner should be removed to keep

the other trees healthy.

2.   Because George will be working late, he will probably be late.

3.   Although I call George a loser sometimes, he is

considered successful by most of his friends.

4.   In order for us to learn about George, we hired a detective.

5.   While I am working in the garden, I usually wear a hat

or cap in order that I might protect my face.

6.   Gardens are always sunny if they are successful.

7.   I have not been a good gardener, for I have lost

the war with the grasshoppers, the brown spot, and the drouth.

8.   No matter how smart you are, you should attend class.

9.   Whatever you learn, you will benefit from it when you write.

10. I will go to see the movie no matter what you say.

11. In order to be given the award, I must attend

the ceremony no matter what excuse I may have.

Lesson 20

Nominal *That* Clauses

Some nominals are clauses. They are introduced by certain connectives. For teaching purposes, I have divided the connectives which introduce these clauses into four groups. The first group has only one member, *that.* Clauses introduced by *that* are quite common and occur most frequently following verbs of thought, certainty, understanding, and emotion. Common verbs preceding them are *know, understand, fear, believe, remember, forget, decide, notice, doubt, hear, learn, expect, say, wish, think,* and *regret.*

$$S \quad V_T \quad DO \ NCI_1 \quad S \quad V_I$$
I know (that you cried.)

$$S \quad V_T \quad DO \ NCI_1 \quad S \quad V_I$$
I believe (that he quit.)

$$S \quad V_T \quad NCI_1 \quad S \quad V_I$$
I understand (that Ted lies.)

That may also be understood but not present.

$$S \quad V_T \ DO \ NCI_1 \quad S \quad V_I$$
I know ({that} you cried.)

$$S \quad V_T \quad DO \ NCI_1 \ S \quad V_I$$
I believe ({that} he quit.)

$$S \quad V_T \quad DO \quad NCI_1 \quad S \quad V_I$$
I understand ({that} he lies.)

Marking Information

When *that* is understood and not stated, I want you to write it in, put wavy lines around it to indicate that it is understood, and then write NCI_1 above it to indicate that it is a pure connective, having no function in the dependent clause,s.

Avoiding Confusion With Other *thats*

That is a word with several functions. Another way to say that is that the spelling *t-h-a-t* is used for several words in English. One introduces nominal clauses, another adjectival and still another an adverbial clause. For example, we have already studied adverbial clauses introduced by the relative nominal *so that*. And we have studied the demonstrative adjectival *that* and demonstrative pronoun *that*.

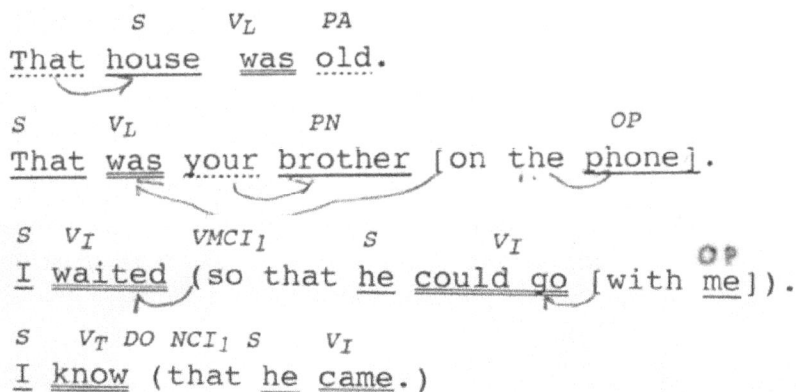

```
          S      V_L    PA
    That house   was   old.

    S    V_L              PN                  OP
    That was  your brother [on the phone].

    S   V_I       VMCI_1    S      V_I           OP
    I waited  (so that  he could go [with me]).

    S   V_T DO NCI_1 S    V_I
    I know (that  he came.)
```

Exercise

Mark the following sentences

1. The   man   said   that   I   was   lying.

2. That   man   lied.

3. That   is   true.

4. So   that   we   would   be   ready,   I   thought   that   we   should   study.

5. I   know   that.

6. I   think   that   that   hat   looks   awful.

7 I   understand   he   lost   his   job   at   the   mall.

8. The   truth   is   that   I   am   happy.

Expletives With Nominal *That* Clauses

Nominal clauses sometimes function as subjects of sentences and come at the first of a sentence.

```
 S  NCI₁ S     V_I                V_L     PA
(That  he  arrived late)  is  possible.
```

But this sounds too formal to most people, so the nominal clause is shifted to the end of the sentence, and the expletive *it* is put in its place at the first of the sentence. Following these changes the sentence above would read

```
 X   V_L     PA        S  NCI₁ S    V_I
 It  is  possible  (that  he  arrived late.)
```

Here is another example of these changes.

```
 S  NCI₁ S     V_I                V_L     PA
(That  he  arrived late) is  possible.
```

Exercise 1

Mark the following sentences. Put an **X** above expletives.

1. It   is   true   that   Harold   won   the   race.

2. That   we   were   sick   was   unfortunate.

3. It   is   regrettable   that   you   made   that   mistake.

4. That   he   missed   the   bus   is   possible.

5. It   is   certain   that   the   party   will   be   formal.

6. I   know   that   it   is   true   that   Harold   won   the   race.

7. That   he   poisoned   the   weeds   yesterday   is   true.

8. It   is   doubtful   the   senate   will   pass   the   bill   now.

9. He   knows   I   am   his   friend.

10. It   is   shameful   that   we   have   a   rat   in   our   barn.

Exercise 2

Mark the following sentences

1. He   said   that   he   knew   that   you   would   quit.

2. He must have forgotten   that you worked   at that shoe store

for   thirty   years.

3. It   is   certain   that   he   was   sick.

4. I   doubt   that   it   is   certain   that   he   was   sick.

5. The   ring   is   beautiful,   but   it   does   not   appeal   to   me.

6. It   is   the   one   with   the   large   diamond.

7. It   is   truly   beautiful.

8. That   it   is   truly   beautiful   is   true.

9. It   is   true   that   it   is   truly   beautiful.

Lesson 22

Nominal Clauses with *What* Words

Another type of connective also introduces noun clauses. In the sentence

```
S  V_T    DO
I  know  something.
```

the indefinite pronoun *something* may be replaced by a clause introduced by one of these type 2 connectives. Unlike the *that*, these connectives will have a function in the dependent clause.

```
S  V_T   DO S    V_T              DO
I  know  (who  wrestled  the  alligator.)
```

Notice that *who* functions as the subject of the dependent clause. Here's another example.

```
S  V_T    DO DO   S   V_T
I  know  (whom  you  invited.)
```

Notice that the clause *whom you invited* functions as the direct object of *know* and that *whom* functions as the direct object of *invited* inside the dependent clause.

Here are some more examples. In these, the connectives function as adjectivals and adverbials as well as nominals.

```
S   V_T  DO DO   S      V_T
I  know  (what  you  bought.)
```

```
S   V_T  DO DO    S    V_T
I  know  (which  you  liked.)
```

```
S   V_T  DO          DO    S      V_T
I  know  (which  book  you  selected.)
```

```
S   V_T  DO        S    V_T
I  know  (where  you  went.)
```

```
S   V_T  DO        S    V_I
I  know  (when  you  left.)
```

```
  S    V_T   DO      S    V_I
  I   know  (why  you  came.)

  S    V_T   DO      S    V_I
  I   know  (how  you  play.)

  S    V_T   DO          PA    S   V_L
  I   know  (how  strong  you  are.)

  S    V_T   DO              S   V_I
  I   know  (how  hard  you  work.)
```

Here is a list of the second type of connective which introduces noun clauses.

Functioning as nominals inside the clause
who, whom, which, what, whose

Functioning as adjectivals inside the clause
whose, which, what, how

Functioning as adverbials inside the clause
how, where, when, why

Exercise

Mark the following sentences. You shouldn't write NCI2 above these introducers. Instead, you will mark their function.

1. I know who won.

2. I know what you ate.

3. I know why you cried.

4. The teacher thought that you cried.

5. The man knows what he likes.

6. The elephant remembered who hurt him.

7. The plumber knew where he could find the pipes.

8. The telephone company knew who was making the crank calls.

9. He forgot which key opened the door.

10. He understood how brave you were.

Lesson 23

Nominal Clauses Introduced by *Whatever* Words

If you add *ever* to each of the connective words I have called NCI$_2$, then you have the type three connective words. They also have the same kinds of function — *whoever* will be a nominal within the clause and *however* will be an adverbial.

Notice that the clause itself can refer to people and things as well as abstract concepts.

```
   S    S     VI      VT           DO
(Whoever came) brought presents.
```

```
  S    VT  IO  S      VI      DO
I gave (whoever came) a present.
```

```
  S        VT    DO  S      VT                  DO
I will reward (whoever finds my missing dog)
```

```
  S      VI         op  S    VI
I talked [to (whoever came.)]
```

```
  S       DO   S     VT                 Vtp
(Whomever you invite) will be welcomed heartily.
```

```
  S        VT   DO        S       VT       DO
I do not know (whyever he would steal her car.)
```

Exercise

Mark the following sentences.

1. Whoever   finishes   first   leaves   first.

2. I   like   whatever   you ' like.

3. I   like   whatever   happens.

4. I   like   what   happened.

5. I   know   whichever   book   I   should   buy.

6. Whosever   car   that   is   should   be   happy.

7. I   know   that   whatever   he   says   is   true.

Lesson 24

Nominal Clauses Introduced by *Whether or not* or *If ... or not*

The last group of structure words introducing nominal clauses has only two members: *if. . . or not* and *whether . . . or not*. Notice how the clause they introduce may be used as direct objects of a cognitive verb like *know*.

```
  S            VT  DO  NCI4    S        VI  CC  DO   NCI4       S
  I do not know (whether they will go) or (whether they

            VI
  will stay).
```

```
  S            VT  DO   NCI4    S       VI  CC  DO   NCI4        S
  I do not know (whether they will go) or (whether they

            VI
  will not go).
```

```
  S            VT  DO   NCI4    S       VI  CC  DO   NCI4     S
  I do not know (whether they will go) or ({whether they}

       VI
  {will} not {go}).
```

```
  S            VT  DO  NCI4                  S         VI
  I do not know (whether or not they will go)
```

If will work just like *whether* except for this last sentence. It is ungrammatical to write, "I do not know if or not they will go."

Exercise

Mark the following sentences.

1 I did not understand   whether   or   not   Marie   would   be   leaving   alone.

2. He   doesn't   know   if   he   will   go   to   the   play   or   not.

3. He   may   not   have   known   whether   he   would   support   the   group   or   fight   against   them.

4. I   think   that   I   know   what   I   should   do.

Lesson 25

Infinitives As Nominals

Now that we have studied the various kinds of clauses that may answer the question *what,* we can turn our attention to other kinds of structures which can answer that question. We will begin with the nonfinite verbal phrase called an *infinitive* phrase. Perhaps the most fruitful way to begin is to compare nominal clauses beginning with *that* to infinitive phrases.

```
  S    V_T   DO NCI_1   S   V_T              DO
  I   know   (that    he   ate    the  melon.)


  S    V_T  DO SISW   S   ISW   I_T            DO
  I   hate  *for    him   to   eat    the   melon.*


  S    V_T   DO  NCI_1   S    V_I
  I   know   (that    he    left.)


  S    V_T  DO SISW    S    ISW    I_I
  I   hate  *for    him   to   leave.*
```

(Note the way I marked these and employ the same marks in the exercises below. *SISW* stands for subject of infinitive structure word. It is always *for.* Remember that *for* also has two other functions as preposition and coordinating conjunction. *For* is the only *SISW. ISW* stands for infinitive structure word. It is always *to. To* is also a preposition. *To* is the only *ISW.*)

What you see here is very similar to what we studied earlier when we studied adverbial infinitive phrases. Note the word *for,* which is the structure word we observed earlier appearing before the subject of the infinitive. Observe also that the form of the subject of the infinitive is the object form, that the infinitive has the structure word *to* before it, that the remainder of the sentence remains unchanged, appearing just as it does in the clause above it. Let me remind you also that the reason this verbal is called an infinitive is that the phrase indicates no particular time for the action or condition of the verbal. Note that the entire phrase answers the question *what* and not just the infinitive and the *to.* You should mark the beginning of the phrase before the subject of the infinitive structure word when it is present. When the subject of the main verb is the same as the subject of the infinitive, then the subject of the infinitive is understood and omitted along with the structure word. "I hate for me to eat melon" is ungrammatical. We would say, "I hate to eat melon." The infinitive phrase may be in any of your basic patterns. When the infinitive phrase is nominal, you will not be required to write in and mark any understood element. Observe the following sentences and procedures for marking them.

```
       S  V_T   DO ISW  I_I
1. I hate ‡to work.‡


       S  V_T   DO SISW   S   ISW    I_I
2. I hate ‡for Susan to work.‡


       S  V_T   DO ISW  I_T  IO     DO
3. I hate ‡to give you trouble.‡


       S  V_T   DO ISW  I_T  DO      OC
4. I hate ‡to call you silly.‡


       S  V_T   DO SISW  S  ISW  I_L    PA
5. I hate ‡for you to be silly.‡


       S  V_T   DO SISW  S  ISW  I_L      PN
6. I hate ‡for you to be a teacher.‡


       S  V_T   DO SISW  S  ISW  I_L    PA
7. I hate ‡for you to be sick.‡


       S  V_T   DO SISW  S  ISW      I_TP
8. I hate ‡for you to be attacked.‡
```

Exercise

Mark the following sentences.

1. I like to wash my dog.

2. I would like for you to wash my dog.

3. I know he washed the dog.

4. When he tried to remove the burr, the dog whined.

5. He started to get personal, and they objected to his behavior.

6. They went to town to buy some milk for the children, for

they hate for them to be thirsty.

Lesson 26

The Infinitive Phrase as Subject

Just as *that* clauses were more formal as subjects, so also is the infinitive phrase. And just as with those clauses, the infinitive phrase can be moved to the end and be replaced by the expletive *it*. Consider these similarities.

```
S NCI₁ S   V_T            DO      V_L  PA
(That I stole the purse) was bad.
```

```
X   V_L  PA  S NCI₁ S   V_T           DO
It was bad (that I stole the purse.)
```

```
S SISW S ISW   It       DO    V_L  PA
‡For me to steal the purse‡ was bad.
```

```
X   V_L  PA S SISW S  ISW   It          DO
It was bad ‡for me to steal the purse.‡
```

If the subject of the infinitive is unimportant or general, it may be omitted.

```
S ISW  It      DO    V_L  PA
‡To steal purses‡ is bad.
```

```
X   V_L  PA S ISW It    DO
It is bad ‡to steal purses.‡
```

Exercise

Mark the following sentences.

1. It is smart to leave the party early.

2. To be a hero is not very difficult if you are brave and talented.

3 To be early for my appointments, I must start to get ready quite soon.

4. It is possible for me to arrive somewhere early.

5. I wanted to buy a car, so I priced one, but it was too expensive.

6. It is unlikely that I will buy it now.

Lesson 27

Infinitive Phrase Without Structure Words

When the infinitive phrase is the object of certain verbs, the subject of the infinitive structure word *for* is omitted and the first word of the infinitive will probably be the first word of the noun phrase functioning as the subject of the infinitive. So there will be no structure word to indicate where the phrase begins. We must depend instead on recognizing which verbs govern their infinitive phrase objects without *for*. There are some variations in usage with these verbs. For example, I could say *I expect for him to eat the melon* or *I expect him to eat the melon*. I and most of my students would say *I want him to eat the melon*. But I have had some students who insisted that they would say *I want for him to eat the melon*. Observe the following sentences.

```
   S   V_T    DO SISW  S   ISW   I_I
   I  hate  ‡ for  him  to  leave.‡
```

```
   S   V_T    DO S  ISW   I_I
   I  want  ‡him  to  leave.‡
```

```
   S   V_T    DO ISW   I_I
   I  want  ‡ to  leave.‡
```

The Infinitive Phrase After Indirect Object

The structure word *for* also will not appear at the first of an infinitive phrase when an indirect object appears before the phrase. Few verbs can take both an indirect object and an infinitive phrase as the direct object. Two of them are *ask* and *tell*. Consider these sentences.

```
   S    V_T            DO
   I  said        something.
```

```
   S    V_T  IO        DO
   I  told  him   something.
```

```
   S    V_T  IO  DO NCI1  S           V_T    DO
   I  told  him ( that  he  should eat  apples.)
```

```
   S    V_T         DO SISW  S   ISW   I_T    DO
   I  said       ‡ for  him  to  eat  apples.‡
```

```
 S     VT    IO DO  SISW  S ISW    IT      DO
*I told him  ‡  for him  to  eat  apples.‡
```

```
 S     VT   IO  DO   ISW  IT     DO
I told him  ‡  to  eat  apples.‡
```

```
 S     VT      IO   DO SISW  S  ISW  IT       DO
*I asked him   ‡ for him  to  eat  apples.‡
```

```
 S     VT    IO             DO ISW   IT     DO
I asked him              ‡  to  eat  apples.‡
```

Of course what is happening here is that the two ungrammatical sentences marked with the asterisks have indirect objects which are the same as the subject of the infinitive. When that occurs, we must delete the subject of the infinitive and with it the *for*, so we are left with the structure word *to* to mark the *beginning* of the phrase. But now it looks much like the sentences with the verbs *want* and *expect* in the sentences above. The only way we can tell these apart and mark them correctly is to watch for the verb which precedes the infinitive phrase. If we watch these verbs, we will know that when preceded by *want* the noun or pronoun is in the infinitive phrase, and when preceded by *ask* the noun or pronoun is outside.

```
 S    VT  DO   S   ISW     Ii
I want ‡  him to  leave.‡
```

```
 S    VT     IO DO ISW    Ii
I asked him ‡ to  leave.‡
```

Exercise 1

Mark the following sentences.

1. I expect him to forget her

2. I told Margie to buy the hat.

3. I went to town to buy the hat.

4. I hate for her to buy that outlandish hat.

5. I asked him to be quiet about his discovery until he got his patent.

6. When he agreed to remain quiet, I was glad.

Under certain circumstances the structure word *to* may not be there to help us recognize the infinitive phrase as direct object. The most common circumstance is following some verbs of the senses. Notice how these sentences are marked.

```
S   V_T    DO   NCI_1  S    V_I
I  know  (  that   he  left.)
```

```
S   V_T  DO NCI₁  S         V_I
I  know  ((that)  he        left.)
```

```
S   V_T    DO    S      ISW   I_I
I  wanted        ‡him  to  leave.‡
```

```
S    V_T  DO SISW   S   ISW     I_I
I  said ‡ for   him  to  leave.‡s
```

```
S    V_T  IO   DO  ISW   I_I
I  told  him  ‡  to  leave.‡
```

```
S   V_T    DO   S      I_I
I  saw   ‡ him  leave.‡
```

```
S  V_T    DO   S     I_I
I  heard  ‡him  leave.‡
```

Notice particularly the difference between the second sentence and the last one. The difference between the clause with the understood *that* and the infinitive phrase cannot be determined by structure words. So to recognize the structure, we must remember that verbs of the senses such as *heard* will not be followed by phrases containing the structure words. In that case we must look even more carefully at the verbal and notice the absence of an ending and notice that the subject of the infinitive must be in the object form if it is a pronoun. If the subject is not a pronoun, we can make a quick mental substitution to see what it would be. For example, if we have the sentence *I saw the boy leave*, we could check to see whether *he* or *him* would be the pronoun which fits the structure. If it is *him*, the structure is an infinitive phrase rather than a clause.

In addition to the verbs of the senses — *see, hear, feel, watch, listen to* — there are a few verbs which may be followed by infinitive phrases without structure words — *let, help, make,* and *have*.

```
S  V_T  DO  S  It        DO
I  let  ‡him eat  the  melon. ‡
```

```
S  V_T  DO  S  It        DO
I  had  ‡him eat  the  melon. ‡
```

```
S  V_T  DO  S  ISW  It      DO
I  had  ‡him  to  eat  the  melon. ‡
```

```
S    V_T    DO  S  It        DO
I  helped  ‡him eat  the  melon. ‡
```

```
S    V_T    DO  S  ISW  It      DO
I  helped  ‡him  to  eat  the  melon. ‡
```

Some speakers employ *to* after *have* and *help*.

Exercise 2

Mark the following sentences.

1. I hate to stop now.

2. I wanted to give Bob a tie.

3. I decided to buy a car.

4. I expect you to understand.

5. I saw him hit the car.

6. I saw that he hit the car.

7. I had him paint my house.

8. I want her to write you a note.

9. I asked her something.

10. I guess the man quit.

11. I watched him quit.

Exercise 3

Mark the following sentences.

1. That man hates to quit early.

2. I know that he saw her fall into the river.

3. This man thinks you are rich.

4. From a distance I could heard him sing, but I could not hear his lyrics.

5. When we were closing, I saw him kiss her .

6. I guess you know which car will win the race.

7. It was dangerous for you to say that Fred hated to be married to Marie.

8. Whoever hates to live alone should not marry.

9. I forgot why he wanted to hear me read.

10. For you to want to own a dog in the dorm was stupid.

Lesson 28

Nominal Infinitive Phrase with What Words

Sometimes the *what* words, NCI2, which introduce noun clauses are used to introduce nominal infinitive phrases. The *what* words function in the same way in these phrases as they did in the clauses. Here are the example of clauses introduced with *what* words that I used in Lesson 22.

```
 S   Vᴛ  DO DO  S     Vᴛ
 I  know  (what you bought.)

 S   Vᴛ  DO DO   S    Vᴛ
 I  know  (which you liked.)

 S   Vᴛ  DO        DO   S     Vᴛ
 I  know  (which book you selected.)

 S   Vᴛ  DO      S    Vᴛ
 I  know  (where you went.)

 S   Vᴛ  DO      S    Vᴛ
 I  know  (when you left.)
```

Infinitive phrases introduced by *what* words must have the same subject of the infinitive as the subject of the clause to which it is the object. So the subject of the infinitive is omitted.

```
 S     Vᴛ     DO
 I   know  | what    to   buy. |
 S     Vᴛ   DO DO
 I   know  | which   to   like. |
 S     Vᴛ   DO   DO
 I   know  | which book  to   select. |
 S     Vᴛ   DO
 I   know  | where   to   go. |
 S     Vᴛ   DO
 I   know  | when    to   go. |
```

Notice that the *I* who knows the information in the direct object is the one doing the action in the infinitive phrase introduced by the *what* word. The *what* words may be functioning inside the phrase as adjectivals, adverbials, or nominals. We will always mark their function. Because they are connective words they must move to the beginning of the phrase even if they are some kind of object. Notice in the third sentence above that the modifier of *book*, *which*, pulls the object *book* to the front with it.

Exercise 1

Mark the following sentences.

1. I forgot how to tune my car.

2. I remember which marks to use.

3. I know how fast to drive on my road.

4. I don't know where to go tonight.

5. I forget what to call the baby.

6. I don't know whose to borrow.

7. The boy does not know what to give his sister for her birthday.

8. Marie knew why to study for the test.

Exercise 2

Mark the following sentences.

1. I know what she told Mary.

2. She knew what information to give Mary.

3. I hope that he remembers what to do when he goes into the game.

4. I heard what Martha said to Mary about what to feed the baby.

5. I heard the baby cry, but I did not know what to do to stop her.

6. I hope that she remembers to leave me instructions about what I should feed the baby.

7. I want Bill to tell me what to say to George when he arrives from work.

Lesson 29

Present Participle Phrases As Nominals

Of the many structures which answer the question *what* one of the most common is the phrase headed by the verbal ending in *-ing*, called the *present participle*. When the *-ing* verbal heads a phrase functioning as a nominal, it is commonly called a gerund and the phrase a gerund phrase. Whatever we call it, it is highly useful in describing actions. Observe how these sentences are marked.

```
S        V_I                OP
I was talking [about something.]

S        V_I              OP   PrPt           DO
I was talking [about {washing the dishes.}]

S   V_I                    OP
I left [without any money.]

S   V_I            OP   PrPt          DO
I left [without {washing the dishes.}]
```

Notice that in each case the phrase *washing the dishes* answers the question *what?* following the prepositions, *about* and *without*, and so the entire phrase is the object. The structure can serve as other nominals do.

Subject

```
S   PrPt        DO        V_L   PA
{Washing dishes} is important.
```

Direct Object

```
S   V_T   DO  PrPt      DO
I hate {washing dishes.}
```

Predicate Nominal

```
       S    V_L  PN   PrPt          DO
My job is {washing the dishes.}
```

Indirect Object

```
S   V_T   IO  PrPt      DO                DO
I gave {washing my car} my full attention.
```

Notice how the *-ing* structure we have already studied is different from these.

Verb in the Progressive

```
S        VT        DO
I am washing dishes.
```

Exercise

Mark the following sentences.

1. I like floating down the river.

2. Being a king is not easy.

3. I want them to like writing poems.

4. Saying that I was a renegade was unwise.

5. In order for me to finish doing my chores by breakfast, I must arise at dawn.

6. They talked about telling us to quit early.

7. Starting to eat before we get to the table is rude.

Lesson 30

Complementation and Modification of the Participle

Participle phrases may be in any of the nine basic patterns.

```
S   V_T   DO   PrP_T   DO    OC
I  hate  {calling  him  Goober.}
```

```
S   V_T   DO  PrP_L    PA
I  hate  {being  sick.}
```

```
S   V_T   DO  PrPL     PN
I  hate  {being  a  burden.}
```

```
S   V_T  DO  PrPL   PA        OP
I  hate  {being  [in  this  room.]}
```

```
S    V_T  DO      PrPtp
I  hate  {being  beaten.}
```

```
S    V_T  DO    PrPtp            RO
I  hate  {being  given  old  newspapers.}
```

```
S    V_T  DO    PrPtp          ROC
I  hate  {being  called  a  fraud.}
```

```
S    V_T  DO    PrPL         ROC
I  hate  {being  called  silly.}
```

In every case the one who is the subject of the participle is understood to be the same as the subject of the sentence. It would be unnecessary to say *I hate my being beaten.* If the subject of the participle is not the same as the subject, it must be stated.

```
S    V_T        DO  PrPL      PN
I  hate  his  {being  a  burden.}
```

```
S    V_T          DO  PrPt    DO
I  hate  Bob's  {eating  my  cake.}
```

This is considered correct usage. Using the subject of the participle without the possessive marker is not considered standard.

```
*I hate him being a burden.

*I do not like Bob eating my cake.
```

But when the participle phrase is the object of a verb of the senses — *see, hear, feel, watch, listen to* — the possessive marker is not employed even in the most formal usage.

```
 S   V_T  DO  S      PrPi
 I   saw  {him swimming alone.}
```

```
 S    V_T   DO  S       PrPt           DO
 I   heard  {Bob  singing  the  song.}
```

Notice how similar these are to their infinitive equivalents.

```
 S   V_T  DO  S     It
 I   saw  ⁑him  swim  alone.⁑
```

The participle is an interesting hybrid blending some noun qualities with some verb qualities. Sometimes it is more like a noun, sometimes less.

```
 S         V_T                        DO            OP
 I do not like his continuous singing [of that song.]
 S         V_T      PvPT        DO
 I do not like his {singing that song continuously.}
```

When the present participle is more like a noun, an *of* appears before the noun which would normally be the object of the participle.

And, of course, the participle may appear with no complements or modification.

```
 S     V_T     DO
 He  liked  swimming.
```

```
  S      V_L    PA
 Eating  is  important.
```

Exercise 1

Mark the following sentences.

1. I   quit   talking   in   class.

2. He was talking about dropping English.

3. His task is painting the ceiling.

4. Painting the ceiling blue should be easy.

5. He is crying.

6. Bob has been writing letters to Susan.

7. He likes my singing.

8. Being clean is important.

9. I saw him leave.

10. Dancing is interesting.

Exercise 2

Mark the following sentences.

1. I know why he hates washing that dog.

2. Saying that I was a liar was stupid.

3. I know who hates polishing the floor.

4. The people are living near the freeway.

5. The people will continue looking.

6. He tried cooking.

7. He began to like trying to cook.

8. He left without explaining why he did not want us to quit singing our song.

9. I heard him saying that he had watched us win the contest.

Practice 3

Exercise 1

Mark the sentences.

1. Now that I have given Bob whatever he wanted, I wish that I had seen how gluttonous he was.

2. Whichever book he buys will be the wrong one.

3. Whichever book he buys, he will pick the wrong one.

4. No matter where he hides, they will find him because they know where they must look in order to find culprits.

5. Whoever buys a good bicycle will have what he or she needs to arrive economically at his or her destination.

6. I wish that what he told you was the truth.

7. When he said that he knew what I knew, he was lying.

Exercise 2

Mark the sentences.

1. I guess   you can't remember whether or not I told you what I would send you

2. What I said was that I would give you another practice before you took the test.

3. I hope   you gave   what I said your full attention.

4. When Bob was arrested after the party he was given a breathalyzer test in order to discover whether he had been drinking or not.

5. I suspect that the police thought   he was drunk because he was driving wildly.

6. Because of his arrest, he missed class and was given an F on his assignment.

7. No matter what he told the police, they still consider him guilty.

Exercise 3

Mark the sentences.

1. I hope that Bill will learn where he should keep his valuables

2. If Fred is given a raise this week, he will be taking a vacation to Tahiti to rest from his labors.

3. No matter what I am called, I do not become angry because I know I will not be hurt by what someone calls me.

4. In order to be given the award, I must remember what the deadline for entry is.

5. Because of his misbehavior, my dog has been banished to the yard to consider his misdeeds at his leisure.

6. However I feel today, I must write what I know about the mystery of life.

7. Although I know whose bike was stolen by Bill, I will not tell what I know since I am afraid of Bill.

8. It is probable that Hal had been a fascist, but now I think he has become a communist.

9. My friend gave me a cold, and it has lasted a month.

10. No matter how smart he is, he cannot pass unless he learns how he should study.

11. When Bob was sent the letter, he learned when he would receive his award.

12. Whichever person wins the race will be given whatever reward that person wishes

Exercise 4

Mark the sentences.

1. I like giving my children presents.

2. I left without putting the cat out.

3. His removing the child from the well was heroic.

4. I regret leaving home.

5. Washing cars is his main skill.

6. His job is decorating houses.

7. He has been decorating houses for years.

8. Being called a wasp upsets Bob because he is an Irishman.

9. He came here after being fired in Baltimore.

10. Being a grammarian is a very good thing.

11. Riding a bicyle can be economical but tiring.

12. George talked about giving his son a bicycle.

13. Being given a bicycle by his father should please the boy.

14. Being a book thief is not good.

15. He left without saying what he would give his son for the birthday.

Exercise 5

1. I believe that taking test is easy when I study.

2. I know that what he wants is winning the lottery.

3. Although he thinks that I forgot about loaning him

Exercise 4

Mark the sentences.

1. I like giving my children presents.

2. I left without putting the cat out.

3. His removing the child from the well was heroic.

4. I regret leaving home.

5. Washing cars is his main skill.

6. His job is decorating houses.

7. He has been decorating houses for years.

8. Being called a wasp upsets Bob because he is an Irishman.

9. He came here after being fired in Baltimore.

10. Being a grammarian is a very good thing.

11. Riding a bicyle can be economical but tiring.

12. George talked about giving his son a bicycle.

13. Being given a bicyle by his father should please the boy.

14. Being a book thief is not good.

15. He left without saying what he would give his son for the birthday.

Exercise 5

Mark the sentences.

1. I believe that taking test is easy when I study.

2. I know that what he wants is winning the lottery.

3. Although he thinks that I forgot about loaning him the money, I remember that well.

4. Whatever he says about returning the money is probably a lie.

5. No matter where he is working, he hates being given poor tasks.

6. I suspect he has forgotten which train he should take when leaving Paris.

7. I know that owning a home can be expensive, but I will buy one whatever it costs.

8. Being elected President is not easy.

Exercise 6

Mark the sentences.

1. I know that you believe that what I told you was nonsense.

2. It is possible that you forgot calling Bill an old goat, but I don't think he will forget it soon.

3. No matter what you say to apologize, I bet he will still be angry about what you said.

4. Whoever talks to him should try to calm him down, for he has high blood pressure, and it is dangerous for him to be angry.

5. Being called an old goat is not what made him mad, though.

6. I heard him tell his wife that he is mad about your leaving his chain saw in the rain

7. Although you can't remember where you left it, you can't say that you did not know where to put it.

8. Marie and Bob have been having an argument about his watching her make a cake.

Lesson 31

Adjectival Clauses

We have studied several adjectivals:

The adjective in form (before the noun)

$$\begin{array}{ccc} S & LV & PA \\ \end{array}$$
The green bike is pretty.

The determiners (before noun and adjective)

$$\begin{array}{ccc} S & V_T & DO \\ \end{array}$$
The old man grew some green beans.

The prepositional phrase (after the noun)

$$\begin{array}{cccc} S & . & OP & V_L & PA \\ \end{array}$$
The book [on the table] is green.

The possessive noun

$$\begin{array}{ccc} S & V_T & DO \\ \end{array}$$
Bob's car has a flat.

The possessive adjective

$$\begin{array}{cc} S & V_I \\ \end{array}$$
My canoe floats well.

You may have noticed that all of the sentences you have marked have been what are called simple sentences. (They have only one clause since they have a single subject and verb.)

The next adjectival you will meet is a dependent clause, a clause that modifies a noun, called the relative or adjectival clause. Notice that a person might write

$$\begin{array}{ccccccc} S & V_T & DO & & S & V_T & DO \\ \end{array}$$
I bought a house. The house has a green roof.

Either one of these sentences might be embedded in the other to modify the common noun *house*.

$$\begin{array}{cccccc} S & V_T & DO & S & V_T & DO \\ \end{array}$$
I bought a house (which has a green roof.)

$$\overset{S}{\underline{\text{The}}} \quad \overset{}{\underline{\text{house}}} \quad (\overset{DO}{\text{which}} \quad \overset{S}{\text{I}} \quad \overset{V_T}{\text{bought}}) \quad \overset{V_T}{\underline{\text{has}}} \quad \overset{}{\underline{\text{a}}} \quad \overset{}{\underline{\text{green}}} \quad \overset{DO}{\underline{\text{roof}}}.$$

After you embed one clause as a relative clause, the word *house* appears only once in each sentence. The word *which* has been added to replace it. *Which* is the relative pronoun used to replace non-human nouns. *Who* is used to replace human nouns, and *that* may be used to replace either human nouns or non-human nouns. The object form of *who* is *whom*. It is usually used only in formal English, but we will employ it here in order for you to learn how to use it correctly when you wish to.

$$\overset{S}{\underline{\text{The}}} \quad \overset{}{\underline{\text{boy}}} \quad (\overset{S}{\text{who}} \quad \overset{V_T}{\text{rode}} \quad \overset{DO}{\text{my}} \quad \overset{}{\text{bike}}) \quad \overset{V_T}{\underline{\text{left}}} \quad \overset{DO}{\underline{\text{it}}} \quad [\overset{}{\underline{\text{in}}} \quad \overset{}{\underline{\text{the}}} \quad \overset{OP}{\underline{\text{driveway}}}.]$$

$$\overset{S}{\underline{\text{The}}} \quad \overset{}{\underline{\text{man}}} \quad (\overset{S}{\text{that}} \quad \overset{V_T}{\text{coaches}} \quad \overset{DO}{\text{my}} \quad \overset{}{\text{team}}) \quad \overset{V_L}{\underline{\text{is}}} \quad \overset{PA}{\underline{\text{sick}}} \quad \text{today.}$$

$$\overset{S}{\underline{\text{The}}} \quad \overset{}{\underline{\text{boat}}} \quad (\overset{DO}{\text{that}} \quad \overset{S}{\text{he}} \quad \overset{V_T}{\text{built}}) \quad \overset{V_T}{\underline{\text{has}}} \quad \overset{}{\underline{\text{some}}} \quad \overset{DO}{\underline{\text{flaws}}}.$$

In the last sentence the direct object *that* referring to boat is at the first of the adjectival clause rather than at the end as direct objects usually are.

$$\overset{S}{\underline{\text{He}}} \quad \overset{V_T}{\underline{\text{built}}} \quad \overset{}{\underline{\text{the}}} \quad \overset{DO}{\underline{\text{boat}}}.$$

The relative word has a dual purpose. It serves as the direct object and is also a subordinating connective word. As a subordinating connective word, it is at the first of the dependent clause.

Exercise

Mark the sentences as we have been doing in the examples. Put parentheses around the entire adjectival clause and draw a line from the parentheses to the noun that the clause modifies.

1. The boy who borrowed my bike will return it later.

2. The flag which waves above my school disappeared yesterday.

3. Bob bought the bike that I wanted.

4. The boy whom you invited to the party came later.

5. He came late to the party which I gave.

6. A man who is a doctor lives in the apartment which my father bought.

7. The tree that you climbed is tall.

8. A girl who is tall may play basketball.

Lesson 32

Adjectival Clauses With Objects of Preposition First

Any noun in the dependent clause may be replaced by the connective word, not just the subject or direct object. In the following sentence, the object of the preposition is replaced by a relative pronoun.

```
            S      OP    S    VI                        VL     PA
The  room  (which  I  walked  [into        ])  was  empty.
```

```
            S              OP    S   VI     VL    PA
The  room  ([into  which]  I  walked)  was  empty.
```

The structure is the same for each adjectival clause. They mean the same.

```
  S    VI                  OP
I  walked  [into  the  room.]
```

The second sentence is more formal, but few people I know would use it except in very formal written English.

Another possibility also exists. In English, if the relative pronoun is functioning as an object it may be omitted:

```
The room I walked into was empty.
```

In marking this type of sentence, always write in the omitted relative pronoun object and put wavy lines on either side of it to indicate that it was not written but was understood to be there.

```
            S        OP    S    VI                  VL     PA
The  room  (which  I  walked  [into    ])  was  empty.
```

Here is another example.

```
            S     DO    S    VT     VL    PA
The  man  (whom  you  called)  was  sick.
```

Omit the relative pronoun, and you get

```
The man you called was sick.
```

This sentence would be marked as follows:

The man (without you called) was sick.

Exercise

Mark these sentences.

1. The people   you invited came to the party.

2. He knows the mechanic   you hired.

3. The park at which you played was attractive.

4. The lot   you parked in has an attendant.

5. The lifeguard whom you know waved to us.

6. The people who lived here during the winter left a message which

we must find.

Lesson 33

Adjectival Clause With Relative Adverbials and Adjectivals

In sentences such as

```
           S              OP        S   VᵢII      VᵢII
The restaurant ([in which] we ate) closed.
```

in which is a prepositional phrase meaning *in the restaurant*. The prepositional phrase is an adverbial of place answering the question *where*. The whole prepositional phrase could be replaced by the relative adverbial *where* and the sentence will not change in meaning:

```
        S              S   Vᵢ      Vᵢ
The restaurant (where we ate) closed.
```

The relative adverbial *where* can only be used following a noun which refers to a place. Notice that the clause is still adjectival even though it is introduced by an adverbial. There are two other relative adverbials: *when* and *why*.

```
        S         OP      S    Vᵢ      Vₗ    PA
The day ([on which] he arrived) was beautiful.
```

```
        S         S    Vᵢ      Vₗ    PA
The day (when he arrived) was beautiful.
```

```
        S            OP    S   Vᵢ     Vₗ    PA
The reason ([for which] he came) was wrong.
```

```
        S          S   Vᵢ    Vₗ    PA
The reason (why he came) was wrong.
```

The relative adverbial *when* replaced the adverbial prepositional phrase *on which*. The relative adverbial *when* can only follow a noun which refers to time such as *moment, minute, hour, day, week*, or *year*. The relative adverbial *why* can only be used following the word *reason*.

Exercise 1

Mark the following sentences.

1. The place where we entered was open today for some reason.

2. The day when I hit the long double was the day when I became a hitter.

3. The reason why he left is unclear.

4. The moment at which he arose was important.

5. The boy who sat on the table broke its leg.

6. Tom knows the day when the store gets the watermelons.

7. I know the spot where the wreck occurred.

There is one other relative word: the relative adjectival *whose*. *Whose* is used to refer to possessive nouns.

$$\begin{array}{ccccc} S & S & V_T & DO & V_I \\ \text{The boy (whose sister won the race) cheered loudly.} \end{array}$$

Whose, of course, replaces "the boy's" in the dependent clause:

$$\begin{array}{ccc} S & V_T & DO \\ \text{The boy's sister won the race.} \end{array}$$

The words *who/whom, which,* and *that* will function as nominals in dependent adjectival clauses. The words *where, when,* and *why* will function as adverbials, and the word *whose* will function as an adjectival.

Exercise 2

Mark the following sentences.

1. The boy who lives near the pond skates there during the winter.

2. The goats which you sold ran away.

3. The carpenter whose tools are sharp can do good work.

4. Carolyn likes the cafe where they serve the delicious shrimp.

5. A man I know won the contest during the festival.

6. The car which I wrecked is a pile of junk now.

7. Lettuce   is   a   vegetable   I   like.

8. I   like   the   driver   whose   car   finished   the   race   first.

Lesson 34

Nonrestrictive Adjectival Clauses

In all of the adjective clauses of the previous lessons, the clauses have been needed to identify the noun modified. Such clauses are called restrictive clauses. Notice how they are different from these.

```
Bob Clements, who lives in Seattle, visited me yesterday.

Our catcher, who had been sick, made an error.
```

In these cases the subjects *Bob Clements* and *Our catcher* have already been identified without the aid of the adjectival clauses. The clauses provide additional information about the nouns they modify. The relative words *that, when,* and *why* are not used to introduce non-restrictive clauses. In speech there is always a pause before and after a non-restrictive clause. The restrictive clause does not have a pause before it, but may have one after it. The non-restrictive clause is set off by commas.

Exercise 1

Mark the following sentences.

1. Margie, who lives across the street, plays the drums after midnight.

2. Ft. Worth, where the west begins, is a large city now.

3. The Sabine river, which flows from the North, is the Eastern boundary of Texas.

4. My son, who likes mysteries, loves your book.

Exercise2

Punctuate the following sentences by placing commas around non-restrictive adjectival clauses.

1. Mary Casper who had been our president talked yesterday at our meeting

2. The tree that he cut was sick.

3. The time when he came was inappropriate.

4. He hit Carolyn Tobin who was innocent.

5. Mom who loves animals hated my cute, little snake.

Lesson 35

More about Adjectival Clauses

When, once, and *where* can introduce adjectival clauses, nominal clauses, and verb-modifying clauses. We can still tell which is which by noticing word order and seeing what question the structure answers.

```
 S   V_T  DO            OP   S   V_I
 I  know  ([at what time] he came.)  What?

 S   V_T  DO      S    V_I
 I  know  (when  he  came.)  What?

        S           OP   S   V_I   V_L   PA
 The  time  ([at which] he came)  was  early.    Which time?

        S          S   V_I   V_L   PA
 The  time  (when  he came)  was  early.    Which time?

   S    V_I
 Bob  came  then.    When?
```

Adjectival clauses can modify any noun in any structure. Since adjectival clauses have nouns in them, adjectival clauses may appear within other adjectival clauses. And in turn they may appear in still other adjectival clauses.

```
        S    S    V_T      DO       DO   S   V_T     V_L       PN
 The  boy  (who bought the bike (which I sold))  is  my  friend.

        S     DO   S    V_T                     OP          S
 The  tree  (which we brought [from the spot (where it

        V_I   V_L  PA                OP
 grew)])  is alive now [in our yard.]

 S   V_T      DO      S    V_T         DO       S   V_T
 I  met the man (who gave the lessons (which had the

            DO        DO  S   V_T
 information (that I wanted.)))
```

All of the modifiers of the object of the preposition are in the prepositional phrase.

```
 S     V_I               OP        DO    S    V_T
He  went  [to the  cafe  (which  we  liked.)]
```

Exercise

Mark the following sentences.

1. We scared the deer which were eating the vegetables that we had planted in the spring.

2. I saw the man who had the car which had the bumper which had the sticker which had the letters that glowed.

3. The plumber that the mechanic who fixed our car recommended fixed our pipes.

4. The cornerback tackled the end who had received the pass which the quarterback threw

Lesson 36

Present Participles Phrases As Adjectivals

Both restrictive and nonrestrictive adjective clauses can often be shortened and still accomplish the same purpose. Notice the nature of the changes to the following sentences.

The man (who was clacking his false teeth so loudly) was my father.

The man {clacking his false teeth so loudly} was my father.

The people (who are standing [in line] so long) are getting weary.

The people {standing [in line] so long} are getting weary.

The man (who is being so obnoxious) is not a friend [of mine].

The man {being so obnoxious} is not a friend [of mine].

The people {laughing [at my jokes]} are my friends.

In the first of each of these paired sentences there is a relative pronoun — *who, which,* or *that* — and a form of the verb *be* — *am, is, are, was, were.* In the second these two elements have been deleted. This deletion is called by transformational grammarians the relative-deletion transformation or more commonly t-relative deletion. It will be involved directly in each of the next few lessons. Here we are left with a phrase which is headed by a verb with an *-ing* ending. A verb with this ending is, of course. called a *present participle,* so this verb phrase is called a present-participle phrase. It has the same adjectival function as the relative clause which it replaced.

Notice that any of your nine basic patterns can still occur in the present participle phrases. The participle can be linking, intransitive, transitive, or transitive passive.

Exercise

Mark the sentences following the method used in the example above.

1 The   people   who   are   swimming   in   the   swift   water   must   be   careful.

2. The   dog   barking   at   the   postman   is   a   nuisance.

3. The   people   eating   the   popcorn   so   loud   are   sitting   behind   me.

4. I   talked   to   the   men   being   given   the   award   about   their   honor.

5. The   dog   being   a   nuisance   is   my   dog.

6. The   man   giving   the   children   the   balloons   is   George   Ogilvie.

7. The   people   who   have   been   staying   here   may   be   leaving   soon.

8. I   want   one   of   the   pies   cooling   on   the   top   shelf   of   the   pie   safe.

Lesson 37

Past Participles As Adjectivals

The two sentences below have essentially the same meaning.

```
The student who was punished by the principal cried.
The student         punished by the principal cried.
```

The first sentence contains an adjectival clause with a transitive passive verb:

The student (who was punished [by the principal]) cried.

The second sentence contains the phrase *punished by the principal* which serves the same purpose as the adjectival clause; it modifies *the student*. Its head word is a past participle indicated here by the *-ed* ending. We will mark the past participle phrase in the following manner.

The books <stacked [on the floor]> were old.

I know the man <elected president.>

Notice how the following sentences are related.

1. Somebody stacked the books [on the floor.] They were old.

2. The books were stacked [on the floor.] They were old.

3. The books (which somebody stacked [on the floor]) were old.

4. The books (which were stacked [on the floor]) were old.

5. The books <stacked [on the floor]> were old.

Exercise 1

Mark the following sentences. Convert the adjectival clause to a past participle phrase, then mark the resulting sentence. Use number one as an example.

1a. The man (who was attacked [by the lion]) died.

1b. The man <attacked [by the lion]> died.

2a. The trees which were chopped by the lumberjacks yesterday have been towed away.

3a. Sylvia admired the poems which were written by her friend.

4a. Fred hated the man who was elected president.

5a. The man who was given the award smiled broadly.

Exercise 2

Mark these sentences.

1. The people packed into the stadium had watched a great game.

2. I think that the people who were sent the invitation enclosed in the blue envelopes came to the party.

3. The pies eaten by the contestant were tasteless.

4. The trees cut by Bill were used for posts.

5. The student elected cheerleader by the judges chosen by the students were seniors.

Lesson 38

Appositives As Adjectivals

In the previous two lessons, we have been working with adjectival constructions which tell what someone is doing or what is being done to someone. Additionally, there are adjectival clauses which have the **S V$_L$ PN** pattern and which have the purpose of placing the word modified into a group, to give it a name.

```
          S       S    VL                         PN          VI
John Carson, (who was a well-known painter), died alone
                OP
[in his sleep].
```

```
          S       S    VL       PN                    OP          VI
John Carson, (who was a friend [of George Beasley]), died
                 OP
alone [in his sleep].
```

Notice that these are nonrestrictive clauses which tell more about someone already identified. Just as in the previous two lessons, t-relative deletion can be applied and the *who, which,* or *that* and the *am, is, are, was,* or *were* can be deleted. The predicate nominal from the clause now becomes an appositive.

```
          S            App     VI
John Carson, a well-known painter, died alone
          OP
[in his sleep].
```

```
          S       APP                 OP          VI
John Carson, a friend [of George Beasley], died
               OP
alone [in his sleep].
```

The word *appositive* comes from **position** and **ad**—*beside*. Because the appositive phrase is what remains of an adjectival clause which comes immediately after the noun being modified, the appositive phrase is after the noun being modified. So it is named for its usual position beside the noun.

Some people confuse the appositive with the object complement. Notice the difference in these two sentences when they are converted to passive voice.

```
           S        VT      DO     OC
His friends considered him a fool.
```

```
        S     VT      DO              App
My sister saw Tom Cruise, the actor.
```

```
    s          VTP         ROC                OP
He was considered a fool [by his friends].

            s              App         VTP          OP
Tom Cruise, the actor , was seen [by my sister].
```

Exercise

Mark the following sentences.

1. We elected Tim captain.

2. I talked to Hiram Golightly, the custodian, about the bad light.

3. Boston, sometimes called Bean town, is the home of the Red Sox.

4. Bill Smith, whose friend, George Brown, owns a boat, often borrows it.

5. I consider Millicent Pembroke, our guide, a stuff shirt.

6. George Carson, who called himself the magnificent one, is
a miserable failure.

7. Somebody gave George, our captain, the answers to the test.

8. I was replaced in the third inning by Bill Van Fleet,
a wild lefthander who had lost his last three games.

9. My car, an old Olds, runs well on unleaded gas, a product sold everywhere.

10. He climbed the tree, a task easily accomplished.

Adverbs of Location As Predicate Adjectives

We have already seen examples of how the location of something can be used to identify it.

```
       S              OP      V_L  PN
The book [on the desk] is mine.
```

```
       S                V_T        DO
The people here must do the job alone.
```

On the desk and *here*, though more often used as adverbials, are in these examples functioning as adjectivals because they are modifying nouns. We know which book the speaker of this sentence is claiming. We know it is not the one anywhere else but on the desk. Similarly, we can use location in the predicate adjective position to modify a noun.

```
    S       V_L    PA
The people are here
```

```
    S    V_L  PA         OP
The book is [on the table}.
```

Some grammarians refer to these as adverbials, but when you are classifying words and phrases by function, they should be considered adjectivals and following linking verbs, they will, of course, be predicate adjectives. Often, through frozen metaphors, location words and phrases serve a more obvious adjectival function.

```
 S   V_L  PA           OP
Bill is [out of his head].
```

```
 S    V_L  PA          OP
Tim is [on the wagon].
```

Exercise

Mark the following sentences

1. Helen   has   been   here   lately.

2. Joe   is   in   the   pool   now.

3. The people in the pool are in the shade.

4. I am running away to my Uncle's house.

5. Chuck is in the dumps.

6. Gloria is on top of the world.

7. The people swimming in the deep water are in trouble.

8. Harry Bartlett, my doctor in Austin, is an osteopath.

Lesson 40

The Infinitive as Adjectival

We have seen in previous lessons that infinitive phrases could be adverbial, answering the question *why*, or nominal, answering the question *what* as in these examples.

Why did I save money?

I saved money in order for my family to take a vacation.

What do I hate?

I hate for my family to waste money.

Infinitive phrases can also be used as modifiers of nouns. They parallel some adjectival clauses expressing obligation.

The following two sentences can be combined because they have a common noun, man.

We should elect the man mayor.

The man is Bill Thigpen.

The sentence we get if we imbed the first into the second is

The man (whom we should elect mayor) is Bill Thigpen.

Since the introducer of the adjectival clause is an object, if we wish, we can delete it, but we don't have to. It is not a required deletion in English.

```
The man we should elect mayor is Bill Thigpen.
```

When we mark these, we show that the connective word is understood by writing it in and putting wavy lines around it.

The man (whom we should elect mayor) is Bill Thigpen.

The infinitive phrase as an adjectival can be used instead of the clause.

We can change the first sentence into an infinitive phrase by taking the modal auxiliary *should* out and replacing it with a *to*. Because the subject is a pronoun, we change it to an object form and place a *for* in front of it.

```
For us to elect the man president.
```

But when we imbed it, we see how the infinitive phrase is different. With the adjectival clause, we could leave the common element *whom* in the sentence or delete it. With the infinitive phrase, we have no choice. We have to delete the common element. So we delete the man and get

The man [for us to elect mayor] is Bill Thigpen.

Here are a few more examples of how this works and how we will mark them.

You should buy Sarah the ring.

The ring is the one [with the big diamond.]

The ring (which you should buy Sarah) is the one [with the big diamond.]

The ring [for you to buy Sarah] is the one [with the big diamond.]

Here is an example where the common noun is the object of the preposition *to*.

He should give a diamond ring [to the girl.]

I know the girl.

I know the girl ([to whom] he should give the ring.)

I know the girl (whom he should give the ring [to.])

I know the girl (he should give the ring [to.])

I know the girl [for you to give the ring [to.]]

In the last two sentences, the preposition has to stay at the end of the infinitive phrase and cannot be moved forward as it was in the *to whom* example. In marking, we will add the noun phrase which is common to both clauses. So even though deleting *the girl* from the insert sentence is obligatory, *the girl* is still understood to be the object of *to*.

Exercise

Mark the following sentences.

1. I know the car that you should give me.

2. I know the car for you to give me.

3. The girl we should choose captain is Michelle.

4. The girl for us to choose captain is Michelle.

5. The people who will be given the prize are happy.

6. The people to be given the prize are happy.

7. The race for us to win is the 10K.

8. The room for us to work in is the kitchen.

9. The character for me to be is Hamlet.

Lesson 41

Clauses Complementing Predicate Adjectives

There are clauses which are in form like nominal clauses because they are introduced by a *that* which has no function in the clause. But these clauses complement a certain kind of predicate adjective.

I am afraid (that he will hit me.)

I am sure (that he lied.)

I am certain (that he lied.)

Some of the predicate adjectives which may be complemented by these clauses are *sure, certain, scared, ashamed, afraid, mortified, confident, assured, fearful, mad, angry, enraged, hopeful*. These adjectivals express certainty, doubt, or an emotion.

Infinitives Complementing Predicate Adjectives

Some of these words may also be complemented by infinitives.

I am afraid *for him to leave here early.*

I am afraid *to go.*

I am sure *to win.*

In these examples, the subject of the infinitive and its structure word *for* are omitted if the subject of the infinitive is the same as the subject of the main clause. With words like *sure* and *certain* the only possible subject of the infinitive is the same as that of the main clause. So with *sure* and *certain* as predicate adjectives, any following infinitive phrase will not have a subject of infinitive or subject of infinitive structure word.

Avoiding Confusion With Extraposed Subject

Both the clausal and infinitive complements are sometimes confused with extraposed nominal clauses and nominal infinitives.

X V$_L$ PA   S NCl S V$_I$
It <u>is</u> possible (that <u>he</u> <u>lied</u>.)

S V$_L$ PA NCl S V$_I$
I <u>am</u> not <u>sure</u> (that <u>he</u> <u>lied</u>.)

S S V$_I$ V$_L$ PA
(That <u>I</u> <u>lied</u>) <u>is</u> possible.

*That I lied is not sure.

S V$_L$ PA IW I$_I$
I <u>am</u> <u>afraid</u> ‡to <u>go</u>.‡

X V$_L$ PA   S IW I$_I$
It <u>is</u> <u>dangerous</u> ‡to <u>go</u>.‡

*To go is afraid.

S IW I$_I$ V$_L$ PA
‡To <u>go</u>‡ <u>is</u> <u>dangerous</u>.

The confusion can be cleared up easily if you attempt to move the clause or phrase to the subject position. If it cannot be moved, then it is not an extraposed subject.

Exercise

Mark the following sentences.

1. I am scared that Bo will arrive early.

2. He is confident that I can win.

3. It is doubtful that I can win.

4. He is doubtful that I can win.

5. I am certain that I will win.

6. I am certain to win.

7. It is certain that I will win.

8. I know that I will win.

Lesson 42

Intensifying Clauses

Another type of clause which is usually adverbial has the structure word *so* before the word modified and *that* after the word. These clauses usually describe the degree of intensity of the adjective or adverb modified. These clauses frequently figured in the comic routines of Johnny Carson. The straight man asked, "How dumb was he, Johnny?" And Johnny said, "He was so-o-o dumb that he threw himself to the floor and missed."

$$\overset{S}{\text{He}} \ \overset{V_L}{\text{was}} \ \text{so} \ \overset{PA}{\text{unhappy}} \ (\overset{ICI}{\text{that}} \ \overset{S}{\text{he}} \ \overset{V_I}{\text{cried}}.)$$

$$\overset{S}{\text{He}} \ \overset{V_I}{\text{ran}} \ \text{so} \ \text{fast} \ (\overset{ICI}{\text{that}} \ \overset{S}{\text{he}} \ \overset{V_I}{\text{escaped}}.)$$

$$\overset{S}{\text{He}} \ \overset{V_I}{\text{comes}} \ \text{so} \ \text{early} \ (\overset{ICI}{\text{that}} \ \overset{S}{\text{we}} \ \overset{V_{TP}}{\text{are awakened}}.)$$

The structure word *that* is sometimes omitted.

$$\overset{S}{\text{He}} \ \overset{V_L}{\text{was}} \ \text{so} \ \overset{PA}{\text{unhappy}} \ (\overset{ICI}{\text{\{that\}}} \ \overset{S}{\text{he}} \ \overset{V_I}{\text{cried}}.)$$

$$\overset{S}{\text{He}} \ \overset{V_I}{\text{ran}} \ \text{so} \ \text{fast} \ (\overset{ICI}{\text{\{that\}}} \ \overset{S}{\text{he}} \ \overset{V_I}{\text{escaped}}.)$$

Be sure not to confuse these structure words which introduce these intensifying adverbials with these same structure words when they serve other functions. Notice that the word *so* and the *that* clause together modify the word which appears between them. And remember that they work together to answer *how*.

Exercise

Mark the following sentences.

1. Bob is so tired that he has curled up on the floor.

2. I hope that he is not so angry that he will hit me.

3. I am so happy I think I will cry.

4. He hit me, so I cried.

5. I saved money so that I could go to Boston.

6. I guess that I am so mistreated that I should quit.

Lesson 43

Comparative Clauses

Still another kind of clause which modifies adjectives and adverbs is the comparative clause. It too has structure words which will allow you to identify it. Notice the structure words in italics in these sample sentences.

Jim is *more* respectable (*than* George is respectable)

Jim is *as* quick (*as* George is quick.)

Jim is not *so* quick (*as* Bill is quick.)

Jim is *less* angry (*than* Bill will be angry.)

In certain contexts, the structure word *more* is replaced by the suffix *-er. Than* is the introducer of the clause, so I call it a Comparative Clause Introducer and abbreviate that to CCI.

Jim is quicker (*than* Tim is quick.)

In these sentences the linking verb *is* is thought to be followed by the appropriate predicate adjective which is understood but never stated.

Sometimes the verb is also omitted but still is understood.

Jim is quicker (*than* Tim is quick.)

At times the whole verb phrase is replaced by the auxiliary *do.*

Jim runs faster (*than* Bill does run fast.)

Notice that both these and the intensive clauses you studied in the last lesson answer the question *how* before the adjective or adverb of manners.

```
How quick is Jim?
```

S VL PA CCl S VI PA
Jim is quicker (than Tim is quick .)

S VN PA ICl S VT DO
Jim is so quick (that Jim cannot catch him.)

You can obviously distinguish the intensive clause from the comparative one because the intensive clause is introduced by *that* and the comparative one by *than* or *as*.

Exercise

Mark the following sentences. Write in the understood adjective, adverb, or verb phrase.

1. I run as fast as Bill does.

2. He is not so fast as Bill.

3. I was more disturbed than I have been lately.

4. I do not start as quickly as Fred does.

5. He plays so hard that he grows tired early.

6. Bob is less considerate than Marie is.

Lesson 44

Nouns of Time and Way As Adverbials

Main verbs are always marked for time. The idea of time is also conveyed by adverbs, such as *now, soon, often, frequently.* Sometimes the idea of time can be in a noun used as a nominal, often as the subject of a sentence.

The day was beautiful.

The time [of his arrival] was surprisingly early.

A noun with the concept of time may also function as an adverbial.

He worked that day.

The weather was beautiful that morning.

In these two sentences it is obvious that the noun phrases answer the question *when* and not *what*, and thus are not nominals but adverbials. These nouns may also be modified by adjectivals even though they function as adverbials.

He worked the day (that the storm hit.)

The weather was beautiful the morning (when we took the walk.)

I bought the horse several years ago.

Notice that in the first two sentences in the group above the relative words *that* and *when* both function as adverbials in the dependent clause.

Another noun which may function as an adverbial is *way*. It functions as an adverbial of manner, answering the question *how* or as an adverbial of direction, answering the question **in what direction**.

How does he play?

He plays that way.

He plays the dirty way.

He plays the way (that I play.)

Notice that in the last sentence the relative word *that* functions as an adverbial in the dependent adverbial clause because it refers to the way he plays.

Exercise

Mark the following sentences.

1. He came yesterday.

2. He . left today.

3. He will return the day that we paint the barn.

4. I will finish college next semester.

5. He will leave the second that he finishes.

6. The day that he arrived was beautiful.

7. He walks that way intentionally.

8. The man will complete the task the month after the election.

9. I forgot to buy a newspaper this morning.

10. The morning when it snowed I was in New York.

11. The way you walk is silly.

12. You walk in a silly way.

Nominative Absolutes and Present Participles as Adverbials

Manner adverbials answer the question *how*. The most common manner adverbial is an adverb in form, having the *-ly* added to a word with an adjective ending, for example *carefully, cautiously, quickly*. Often a prepositional phrase will serve as an adverbial of manner, for example, *with care, with caution, with quickness.*

He works cautiously.

He works [with caution.]

With is a preposition which may also introduce a phrase which functions to describe accompaniment or instrumentality.

He works [with Fred.]

He works [with a hoe.]

The idea of *how* is a broad concept which can include both accompaniment and instrumentality. It can even be extended to include the idea of accompanying actions.

He walked in [with his feet {clomping loudly.}]

He walked in, {clomping loudly [on the wooden floor.]}

He walked in, his feet {clomping loudly.}

Each of these sentences has a phrase following the place adverbial *in* which functions as an adverbial of manner. The first is a prepositional phrase, the second a present participle phrase, and the third is a nominative absolute.

A nominative absolute is a construction that usually describes some action or condition simultaneous with the action or condition in the main clause. The two constructions share the same context. Nominative absolutes are much like present participle phrases as the last two examples above show. Nominative absolutes are frequently modified by past participles, adjectives, and location structures.

He stood there, his hands tucked [in his pockets].

He stood there, his hands dirty [from hard work.]

He stood there, his hands [in his pockets.]

Exercise

Mark the following sentences. Write NA above the nominative absolute.

1. He watched the game, staring intently at every play.

2. The people were dancing enthusiastically, their feet beating wildly in the red dust.

3. They came to the party with their jeans tucked in their outlandish boots.

4. I attended college, hoping that I would have enough money to finish.

5. He came to the party, wearing rings in his nose, his hair dyed indigo.

6. Whoever wants to know what Bob wants must follow him daily, hanging on his every word.

7 His boots unshined, his hair streaming wildly, his hand holding his hat high above his head, he rode into the ballroom, still smiling his silly way.

Lesson 46

Past Participle as Nominal

We have previously studied present participle phrases as nominals. It is relatively rare, but a past participle phrase can serve as a nominal also.

    I saw the car wrecked by John.

This is an ambiguous sentence. There are two possible meanings depending on whether the phrase is considered nominal or adjectival. Notice the two ways of marking it.

I saw the car <wrecked [by John.]>

I saw <the car wrecked [by John.]>

Marked the way the first one is, it means that after the wreck I saw a car and identified it as the car which had been wrecked. Marked the way the second sentence is, it means that I was there at the scene of the wreck and saw the accident occur. If a pronoun had been used in the first sentence, it would replace both the noun and the following past participle modifier, and the sentence would simply be *I saw it*. Replacing the noun phrase in second sentence would yield, *I saw it wrecked by John.*

Exercise

Mark the following sentences. If the sentence is ambiguous, you may choose which interpretation of the sentence is the correct one.

1. I saw him beaten by the gang.

2. I heard the music played by him.

3. I heard it played by him.

4. I saw him being beaten by the gang.

5. I watched the car be wrecked.

Lesson 47

Compound Auxiliary Verbs

Until now, I have tried to keep verb phrases as uncomplicated as possible by limiting the auxiliary verbs in sample sentences, exercises, and practices to the modals and to the various forms of *do, have* and *be*. But there are several others compound auxiliary verbs that we use more or less often. Probably the most common of these are *be going to* and *have to*. These parallel the modal auxiliaries.

I will go [to the movie] soon.

I am going to go [to the movie] soon.

I must repair the roof.

I have to repair the roof.

Other frequently used compound auxiliary verbs are *used to, ought to,* and *be about to*. Here in Texas, we could not do without *be fixing to*, which we use in place of *be about to*.

Compound auxiliary verbs are sometimes used in combination with other auxiliary verbs in the same verb phrase.

I may be about to have to go.

He might have to work tonight.

He could be going to go soon.

There is a list of compound auxiliary verbs in the word-list appendix.

Exercise

Mark the following sentences. Mark compound auxiliary verbs the way we have other auxiliary verbs — by underlining them twice.

1. He is going to be given the award.

2. He used to want to work to make money.

3. Bob has to stop what he has been saying.

4. I think he is going to be good at marking sentences.

5. Bob has to be working late tonight.

6. Bill will have to complete the book.

Lesson 48

Functions of Infinitive Phrases

Phrases function as a modifier of a verb

These phrases always express a motive, explaining why something is being done

I came [to town] [in order to get a job.]

The introducer of this phrase —*in order*—may be omitted

I came [to town] [to get a job.]

But it can always be understood there. See if you can think in *in order* as a test. Notice that unlike most of the other infinitives, these are movable.

```
In order to get a job,  I came to town.
To get a job,  I came to town.
```

Compare the infinitive of motive to the clause of motive that modifies a verb

I came [to town] (in order that I might get a job.)

In order for or *in order to* introduce adverbial infinitive phrases. *In order that* introduces an adverbial clause.

Phrase functions as nominal

In nominal infinitive phrases that follow certain verbs the structure words *for* and *to* are retained.

I hate [for him to play baseball.]

I like [for him to play baseball.]

Infinitives phrases that follow certain other verbs retain the structure words *to*, but drop the structure word *for*.

```
*I asked him [for him to eat the pie.] (The asterisk indicates
an ungrammatical sentence.)
```

Some verbs followed by infinitive phrases take indirect objects. In these, we drop the *for* and the subject of the infinitive because the subject of the infinitive refers to the same person or thing as the indirect object.

*I asked him | for him to eat the pie. (The asterisk indicates an ungrammatical sentence.)

We are obliged to delete the subject of the infinitive.

I saw him play baseball.

Infinitives that follow certain verbs drop the structure words *for* and *to*. The verbs are *see, hear, feel, smell, watch, listen to, let, help, make,* and *have.*

I saw him play baseball.

I let him play baseball.

Phrase introduced by a conjunction functions as nominal

The type 2 connectives which introduce noun clauses may also introduce infinitive phrases functioning as nominals. Compare these clauses to the parallel infinitive phrases.

I know (what I should give Mary.)

I know what to give Mary

I know (where I should go.)

I know where to go.

Phrase functions as complement to certain predicate adjectives

These predicate adjectives express certainty, doubt, or emotion.

I am sure to go to the movie

I am afraid to go to the movie

I am happy for you to go to the movie

Phrase functions as adjectival

This phrase follows a noun and implies obligation. Notice how in adjectival clauses we may, if we choose, delete the relative nominal when it is an object.

```
        S   /Do  S      Vt        OC  \  Vl      PN
The man (whom we should elect President)  is Bill Johnson.

        S   /Do  S      Vt        OC  \  Vl      PN
The man (that we should elect President)  is Bill Johnson.

        S   /Do  S      Vt    Io  \  Vl      PN
The book (that we should give Tom)  is Tom Jones.

        S   /Do   S      Vt    Io  \  Vl      PN
The book (which we should give Tom)  is Tom Jones.
```

```
The man        we should elect President   is Bill Johnson.

The book        we should give Tom   is Tom Jones.
```

In marking the last two sentences the *whom*, *that*, or *which* should be written in so that you can have the proper pattern in the phrase.

```
        S   /Do    S      Vt        OC  \  Vl      PN
The man ({whom} we should elect President)  is Bill Johnson.

        S   /Do    S      Vt    Io \ Vl      PN
The book ({which} we should give Tom) is Tom Jones.
```

When the adjectival infinitive phrase is used instead of the adjectival clause, there is and obligatory deletion of the word in the dependent clause representing the word being modified.

```
The man  for us to elect     President   is Bill Johnson.
The book for us to give Tom          is Tom Jones.
```

In marking these sentences, you should write in the noun modified by the infinitive phrase, in these cases *man* and *book*.

```
        S  [SisW S isW It {the man}    OC  ] Vl      PN
The man [for us to elect        President| is Bill Johnson.

        S  [SisW S isW It Io {the book} Vl      Do
The book|for us to give Tom         |is Tom Jones.
```

Notice that *President* is an Object Complement and that *Tom* is an indirect object. The words *man* and *book* are necessary to provide the direct objects in order to complete the patterns.

Exercise

Mark the following sentences. Each of the functions listed above are represented at least once.

1. I went   to see   the   movie.

2. I quit   in order that   I   might   stay   with   my   family.

3. To   win,   Bob   would   cheat.

4. I want   to   see   the   movie.

3. I hate   for him   to   see   the   movie.

4. I know   what   I   should   see.

5. I know   what   to   see.

6. I saw   him   go   into   the   movie

7. I know   the   movie   which   you   should   see.

8. I know   the   movie   for   you   to   see.

9. I told   him   to   go   to   the   movie.

10. I stopped   in   order   to   rest.

11. He   is   sure   to   attend   the   lecture.

12. He   is   sure   that   he   will   attend   the   lecture.

Lesson 49

Functions of *That*

Demonstrative Adjectival.

That book is good.

Demonstrative Nominal

That book is good.

Part of a Verb Modifying Clause Introducer, Type 1

Some of these are *so that, now that, in order that, providing that, provided that.*

(So that I could watch the World Series,) I stayed up late.

Sometimes the *that* is omitted

So I could watch the World Series, I stayed up late.

You should write in the *that* when you are marking the sentence.

(So ⸨that⸩ I could watch the World Series,) I stayed up late.

In formal writing, sometimes the *so* is omitted. You don't need to write in the *so* when you are marking the sentence.

(That I might watch the World Series,) I stayed up late.

Noun Clause Introducer, Type 1

I know (that he likes pie.)

Sometimes the *that* is omitted.

I know he likes pie.

You should write in the *that* when you are marking the sentence.

I know (⸨that⸩ he likes pie.)

Adjectival Clause Introducer, a Relative Pronoun

The *that* is used for people or things to replace *who, whom,* or *which* in restrictive clauses.

The sentence diagrams showing:

The book (which he bought) was good.

The book (that he bought) was good.

The boy (who ate the pie) was happy.

The boy (that ate the pie) was happy.

The man (whom she married) was rich.

The man (that she married) was rich.

When the *that* is used as an object in the dependent clause, it may be omitted.

```
The book he bought was good.
The man she married was rich.
```

You should write in the *that* when you are marking the sentence. Or you can write in *which* or *whom*, whichever is appropriate.

The book ({that} he bought) was good.

The man ({that} she married) was rich.

Introducers of Predicate Adjective Complements

I am sure (that he ate the pie.)

Sometimes the *that* is omitted.

```
I am sure  he ate the pie.
```

You should write in the *that* when you are marking the sentence.

He is so tired (that he is slee

Working with *So* in introducing Clauses which Qualify or Intensify Adjectives and Adverbs.

Sometimes the *that* is omitted.

```
He is so tired he is sleeping in his clothes.

He works so hard he often becomes ill.
```

You should write in the *that* when you are marking the sentence.

Exercise

Mark the following sentences. Each of the functions listed above are represented at least once.

1. When he came here, I was sure that he would wear that tacky hat that he likes.

2. He said that he would wear whatever he liked.

2. I heard that, but I don't believe   what he said was true.

3. That story has been told about him before.

4. I am so confident about his not saying that that I will bet on it.

5. Provided that he avoids wearing that hat, I think   the people that know him will be sure that he has a good time.

6. I don't know   what to say about Bob's running so fast that he lost his shoes.

7. That tree   he climbed was so tall   we could not see him in the high branches.

8. That is not good because being so high is dangerous.

Lesson 50

Functions of *Where, When, Why, and How*

As Question Words

$$\text{Where} \overset{S}{\underset{}{did}} \overset{V_T}{\underset{}{you~buy}} \text{the book?}$$

$$\text{When} \overset{S}{\underset{}{did}} \overset{V_T}{\underset{}{you~buy}} \text{the book?}$$

$$\text{Why} \overset{S}{\underset{}{did}} \overset{V_T}{\underset{}{you~buy}} \text{the book?}$$

$$\text{How} \overset{S}{\underset{}{did}} \overset{V_I}{\underset{}{Tim~work?}}$$

$$\overset{PA}{\underset{}{How~good}} \overset{V_L}{\underset{}{is}} \overset{S}{\underset{}{Tim?}}$$

$$\overset{PA}{\underset{}{How}} \overset{V_L}{\underset{}{is}} \overset{S}{\underset{}{Tim?}}$$

These question words have a function and should be marked accordingly.

As Introducer of Verb Modifying Clauses, Type 1

$$\overset{S}{\underset{}{I}} \overset{V_L}{\underset{}{was}} \overset{PA}{\underset{}{there}} \overset{VMCI}{(\underset{}{when}} \overset{S}{\underset{}{you}} \overset{V_T}{\underset{}{bought}} \text{the} \overset{DO}{\underset{}{book}}.)$$

$$\overset{S}{\underset{}{I}} \overset{V_I}{\underset{}{work}} (\overset{}{\underset{}{where}} \overset{S}{\underset{}{you}} \overset{V_I}{\underset{}{work}}.)$$

Notice that these clauses can be moved to the front and then will be followed by a comma.

$$(\overset{VMCI}{\underset{}{When}} \overset{S}{\underset{}{you}} \overset{V_T}{\underset{}{bought}} \text{the} \overset{DO}{\underset{}{book,}}) \overset{S}{\underset{}{I}} \overset{V_L}{\underset{}{was}} \overset{PA}{\underset{}{there}}.$$

$$(\overset{VMCI}{\underset{}{Where}} \overset{S}{\underset{}{you}} \overset{V_I}{\underset{}{work,}}) \overset{S}{\underset{}{I}} \overset{V_I}{\underset{}{work}}.$$

These connectives have no function in the dependent clauses and should be marked as VMCI1. *Why* and *how* are not this type introducers.

As Introducer of Verb Modifying Clauses, Type 2

$$\overbrace{\text{(No matter how } \underset{S}{\underline{\text{Tim}}} \underset{V_I}{\underline{\text{works}}}\text{,)}} \quad \text{the } \underset{S}{\underline{\text{boss}}} \text{ is } \underset{V_{LP}}{\underline{\text{not satisfied}}}.$$

(No matter how Tim works,) the boss is not satisfied.

(No matter how fast Tim works,) the boss is not satisfied.

(No matter how Tim is,) he complains.

Notice that these clauses can be moved to the rear and will require no comma. These introducers have a function and should be marked accordingly.

As Introducers of Nominal Clauses, Type 2

I know (when you bought the book.)

I know (where you bought the book.)

I know (why you bought the book.)

I know (how Tim works.)

I know (how fast Tim works.)

I know (how Tim is.)

These introducers have a function and should be marked accordingly.

As Introducers of Nominal Infinitive Phrases

I know when to buy the book.

I know where to buy the book.

I know why to buy the book.

These introducers have a function and should be marked accordingly.

As Introducers of Clauses Which Modify Nouns

The time (when he came) was inappropriate.

The place (where he worked) was dangerous.

The reason (why he came) was silly.

These introducers have a function and should be marked as accordingly. *How* is not used to introduce clauses which modify nouns.

Exercise
Mark the following sentences. Each of the functions listed above are represented at least once.

1. I learned when to be quiet.

2. I stopped work when the whistle blew.

3. No matter where I work, I can hear the whistle.

4. The reason why I quit was that I was paid poorly.

5. I learned where the treasure maps were hid.

6. The house where he lived was haunted.

7. I don't know why he quit.

8. The day when I was born was cold.

9. I know when to quit.

10. When Bob arrived at the ranch, the horses had been stolen.

11. I know how to ride.

12. I know how angry he is.

13. No matter how angry he is, he must control his temper.

Lesson 51

Functions of *What, Which, and Whose*

As Question Words

Which book did you buy?

Whose book did you buy?

What book did you buy?

Which did you buy?

Whose did you buy?

What did you buy.

These question words and all of the introducers that follow always have a function in their phrase or clause and should be marked accordingly.

As Introducer of Verb Modifying Clauses, Type 2

(No matter which book you buy) you will not be satisfied.

(No matter which you buy) you will not be satisfied.

(No matter whose book you buy) you will not be satisfied.

(No matter whose you buy) you will not be satisfied.

(No matter what book you buy) you will not be satisfied.

(No matter what you buy) you will not be satisfied.

These question words and all of the introducers that follow always have a function in their phrase or clause and should be marked accordingly.

Introducers of Nominal Clauses, Type 2

I know (which book I should buy.)

I know (which I should buy.)

I know (whose book I should buy.)

I know (whose I should buy.)

I know (what book I should buy.)

I know (what I should buy.)

Introducers of Nominal Infinitive Phrases

I know |which book to buy.|

I know |which to buy.|

I know |whose book to buy.|

I know |whose to buy.|

I know |what book to buy|

I know |what to buy.|

Introducers of Clauses Which Modify Nouns

The book (which I bought) was difficult.

Notice that *which* in this use can only be a nominal. It can be replaced by *that*. Notice also that *which* can be omitted when it is an object. When marking sentences, you will write in the omitted introducer and mark its function.

The book (which I bought) was difficult.

Whose in this use can only be an adjectival

The girl (whose book I bought) has dropped the course.

What does not introduce this kind of clause.

Exercise

Mark the following sentences. Each of the functions listed above are represented at least once.

1.   I think   he knows   whose car to borrow.

2.   The man whose car you borrowed is calling the police.

3.   No matter whose secrets you told, that is wrong.

4.   He knows whose secrets are most important.

5.   I remember which pie you ate.

6.   And you know which I like.

7.   The house   which he bought was haunted.

8.   The note   he printed was libelous.

8.   The house which he lived in was haunted.

9.   The house he lived in   was ugly.

9.   The house   in which he lived was haunted.

10. The house where he lived was haunted.

11. What did he say ?

12. What lesson did you learn?

13. Bess will fire him   no matter what he says.

14. I don't know what to give her.

Practice 4

Exercise 1

Mark the sentences.

1. Now I think that I know who stole the pie from the kitchen.

2. The pie he stole was probably still hot since I had just removed it from the oven.

3. I thought the place where I had stored it was safe, and I figured that I could see whatever happened there.

4. I had not seen my son going into the kitchen, yet I am sure that he must have taken the pie.

5. I do not want to call him a pie thief unless I have some evidence of his taking it.

6. He is so fond of pie that he probably would take it if he had known where I put it.

7. I wish that I had seen him come in last night, so I could know when he came back.

8. The person who took it must have been here between seven and nine in order to have smelled it cooling.

9. It is likely that he came in later without making any noise.

10. But people stealing pies usually do not make a noise however hungry they are.

11. The pie taken from the shelf was a pie which my wife considered wonderful.

12. Pies I bake during the summer are pies treasured for their rarity.

Exercise 2

Mark the sentences.

1. I guess   I should start   keeping better records.

2. Whoever wants to write well   should know what is happening in the world.

3. I am certain that people   that save junk are people   I would like.

4. He works so enthusiastically that he causes the other workers to be eager to work also.

5. While Bob was working for a little money in order to pay his bills, Dan was becoming more famous for gathering the news than Walter was.

6. I heard them say that they wanted to be as good as Dan and Walter were.

7. No matter where he worked, he did the dirty jobs because of his low self esteem, which was communicated in some fashion to the people employing him.

8. He was always in trouble because of his complaining about what he was given.

9. I am afraid to go to the place where I found the body.

10. A person given an award for writing a great book   should be a person   I would respect.

11. A place where you should visit on your vacation is a place   at which good food is served.

Exercise 3

Mark the sentences.

1. Jim stood there, watching the crowd, his eyes constantly moving.

2. He has to be tired after watching the crowd intently so that he will miss nothing.

3. Because he works hard, I think that he is a more careful bodyguard than Bob was.

4. The man to hire for a bodyguard is one who works as carefully as Jim.

5. Jim has been chosen bodyguard of the year as a result of his extraordinarily careful work.

6. I am glad that he was hired to protect the mayor, my brother in law.

7. I am about to watch him work, and I expect him to be as good as they have told me that he was.

8. The mayor wants me to learn how to do what Jim has been doing.

9. I think being a bodyguard as good as Jim is would be so difficult that I would fail.

10. The people attending the rally for the mayor stood in places where Jim could see them easily.

11. The place at which the rally was held was near the city hall.

Appendix 1

Answers to Exercises

Lesson 1

Exercise 1

1. <u>Grover</u>   <u>moaned</u>.

2. <u>The</u>   <u>man</u>   <u>groans.</u>

3. <u>Some</u>   <u>pirates</u>   <u>whistle</u>.

4. <u>Susan</u>   <u>dances</u>.

5. <u>A</u>   <u>child</u>   <u>coughed</u>.

6. <u>Max</u>   <u>quit</u>.

Exercise 2

1. <u>Manuel</u>   <u>is   singing.</u>

2. <u>Some</u>   <u>babysitters</u>   <u>cry</u>.

3. <u>The</u>   <u>dancer</u>   <u>slipped</u>.

4. <u>The</u>   <u>actresses</u>   <u>are   perspiring</u>.

5. <u>The.</u>   <u>roof</u>   <u>was   leaking</u>.

6. <u>The</u>   <u>babies</u>   <u>were   smiling</u>.

Exercise 3

1. <u>The</u>   <u>man</u>   <u>has   stuttered.</u>

2. <u>Gina</u>   <u>lies.</u>

3. <u>Marvin</u>   <u>has   whimpered.</u>

4. <u>The</u>   <u>bandits   have   escaped.</u>

5. The <u>players are coming.</u>

6. The <u>children have finished.</u>

Exercise 4

1. The <u>man will paint</u>.

2. <u>Terry should stop</u>.

3. <u>Elizabeth is whistling</u>.

4. A. <u>paratrooper may jump</u>.

5. <u>Mr. Jones can escape</u>.

6. <u>Harry must start</u>.

Lesson 2

Exercise 1

1. <u>Bob understands now</u>.

2. The <u>girl is leaving tomorrow</u>.

3. The <u>girl will leave tomorrow</u>.

4. The <u>girl leaves tomorrow</u>.

5. The <u>child cried later</u>.

6. <u>Bill ate early</u>.

7. The <u>boy is speaking now</u>.

Exercise 2

1. <u>William was lying here then</u>.

2. The <u>captain may move away soon</u>.

3. <u>Gabby</u>   <u>has</u>   <u>been</u>   <u>sitting</u> up.

4. <u>The</u>   <u>child</u>   <u>will</u>   <u>fall</u>   down now.

Exercise 3

1. <u>The</u>   <u>unhappy</u>   <u>children</u>   <u>were</u>   <u>leaving</u> regretfully.

2. <u>A</u>   <u>young</u>   <u>alligator</u>   <u>moved</u> lazily.

3. <u>The</u>   <u>plumber</u>   <u>fixed</u>   <u>the</u>   <u>pipes</u> clumsily.

4. <u>Bob</u> <u>will</u> <u>polish</u>   <u>the</u>   <u>floors</u> carefully.

5. <u>Some</u>   <u>people</u>   <u>sing</u>   <u>marvelously</u>.

Lesson 3

Exercise 1

1. <u>Malcolm</u>   <u>can</u>   <u>see</u>   <u>the</u>   <u>table</u>   now.

2. The   <u>dog</u>   <u>chased</u>   the   cat   away.

3. The   <u>children</u>   <u>were</u>   <u>teasing</u>   the   horse.

4. <u>Meg</u>   <u>liked</u>   <u>nutmeg</u>.

5. The   <u>workers</u>   <u>were</u>   <u>putting</u>   the   hay   away.

6. The   <u>cat</u>   <u>has</u>   <u>been</u>   <u>eating</u>   the   <u>plants</u>.

7. <u>Charlotte</u>   <u>may</u>   <u>have</u>   <u>been</u>   <u>wearing</u>   the   dress   yesterday.

Exercise 2

1. The *pirates* *carried* the *gold* away.
2. The *people* *spread* out then.
3. The *artist* may be *painting* a masterpiece.
4. The *crab* *grabbed* a *finger*.
5. *Bill* *has* *left*.
6. *Apples* *have* a *core*.

Lesson 4

1. A fortunate *lady* *found* some pretty *rocks* here yesterday.
2. The restive *crowd* *was booing* the lazy *shortstop*.
3. The pesky *kid* *is crying* now.
4. Some smart *people* *eat* green *vegetables*.
5. A swift *runner* *has arrived* early.
6. Some childish *people* *destroyed* the political *poster*.

Lesson 5

1. *I* *have* not *finished* the *work*.
2. *Nobody* *came* early.
3. *Nothing* *works* now.
4. *I* *will* never *hear* the *news*.
5. No *one* *has completed* those difficult *assignments* yet.

Lesson 6

Exercise 1

1. Tom is a carpenter.
   S VL PN

2. The man became a dentist.
   S VL PN

3. Some boys may leave soon.
   S VI

4. Harold threw the ball accurately.
   S VT DO

5. Rover may be a mutt.
   S VL PN

6. The girl remained the captain.
   S VL PN

Exercise 2

1. Ellen has been angry today.
   S VL PA

2. George fought furiously.
   S VI

3. The girl had completed her lessons.
   S VT DO

4. Bill feels sick.
   S VL PA

5. Herbert is a boxer now.
   S VL PN

6. The little girl sat down gracefully.
   S VI

7. The best pies are hot.
   S VL PA

8. The teacher looked excited.
   S VL PA

9. Marvin became a coach.
   S VL PN

10. The man hid the eggs carefully.
    S VT DO

Lesson 7

Exercise 1

1. Elizabeth is happy [in Boston.]
2. The designer ordered the drapes [from Paris.]
3. Bill is a soldier [on Saturday.]
4. Some campers should go [up the mountain] [during the afternoon.]
5. The cats ate the food [on the porch.]
6. The kids were scattering [after the party.]
7. Bob had become ill [before the party.]
8. The horse seemed slow [on the steep trail.]

In sentence number five, "on the porch" could also be interpreted as modifying *food*, telling which food they ate.

Exercise 2

1. The tiger [in the cage] roared.
2. The boy [on the bike] threw the paper [toward the steps [of the house.]]
3. The old trapper had appeared angry [on the first day.]
4. The fans came [through the gates [of the stadium]] early.
5. The man [on the roof] must be careful.
6. An old man shelled some peas [on the back porch] yesterday.
7. The garden [behind the house] was beautiful [in the early morning.]
8. The man [at the gate] took the tickets.

Lesson 8

1. Mr. Simpson sent someone [to the phone.]
2. They had piloted the old barge [down the quiet river.]
3. She raised it sleepily.
4. Bob knew her [at school.]
5. Something is upsetting him.
6. We went [to it] late.
7. He smelled them [near the gate.]
8. The book [on the desk] was covering it.
9. I went [to her] [after the class.]

Lesson 9

1. My shovel is sharp.
2. These books are my books.
3. Ours runs well.
4. Our car runs well.
5. That was a mistake.
6. The dog hid its bone.
7. Those trees are growing tall.
8. I like mine.
9. My cat may be sleeping.

Lesson 10

1. The car was repaired poorly.
2. Calvin was fired yesterday.
3. Bill treated her wound.
4. The tiger has been killed.
5. He has finished his work.
6. He was washing his clothes.
7. These may have been washed already.
8. The jewels were removed [from the vault] [by an expert thief.]
9. He has become a pilot.
10. He was being rewarded well [for his work.]
11. Walt has been the leader recently

Lesson 11

1. Beth mailed her boyfriend some cookies.
2. The clerk handed me my groceries.
3. He gave a bicycle [to me.]
4. The boy sent his girlfriend some flowers.
5. The paperboy tossed me my paper.
6. I was reading the book carefully.
7. They had returned the answers [to the teacher.]
8. Pam mailed her friend a letter.
9. Bob may be angry now.

Lesson 12

1. His employers sent him a check.

2. He was sent a check by his employers.

3. His employers sent a check to him.

4. A check was sent to him by his employers.

5. A check was sent him by his employers.

6. He was mailed a bomb.

7. I have been mistreated by my friends.

8. I may have been handed the receipt.

9. I was being given a haircut by Rudy.

10. Rudy was giving me a haircut.

Lesson 13

1. Bob called me a coward.

2. Harry painted his bike green.

3. Bill made his teacher happy.

4. Gabriel tossed me a hat.

5. I gave Harriet my lemon pie.

6. The senior class chose Mary favorite.

3. Our neighbor has been giving my mother some peaches.

7. Bill may be eating hamburgers in the cafeteria.

8. We selected Clara president of our class.

9. I called Bill a coward.

10. We named our baby Clem.

Lesson 14

1. He was elected cheerleader.
    S   Vbp   ROC

2. He was given a reward.
    S   Vbp   R.O

3. He has been picked as a tax examiner.
    S   Vbp   sw   ROC

4. He has given Susan an award.
    S   Vt   IO   DO

5. They are being elected now.
    S   Vbp

6. We were selecting them yesterday.
    S   Vt   DO

7. He made me mad.
    S   Vt   DO   OC

8. Max's car has been painted red.
    S   Vbp   ROC

9. My car has been clean.
    S   VL   PA

10. My car has been cleaned.
    S   Vbp

11. I always have considered him a fool.
    S   Vt   DO   OC

12. He has always been considered foolish.
    S   Vbp   ROC

Lesson 15

1. My friend ate your apples [during lunch] [at school.]
    S   Vt   DO   OP   OP

2. Bob's horse bit him [on his arm] yesterday.
    S   Vt   DO   OP

3. Your horse runs smoothly.
    S   Vi

4. Mine is clumsy.
    S   VL   PA

5. Your coach is your father.
    S   VL   PN

6. The man [in the car] put his hand out.
    S   OP   Vt   DO

Lesson 16

Exercise 1

1. (When you get here,) we will have a party.

2. I will eat (where he ate.)

3. (Although he was disappointed [by Marie,) he still loves her.

4. (Although he was angry [with her,]) he will forgive her.

5. We quarreled. I haven't seen him since.

6. I will work (if he brings the tools.)

7. (Now that he is rich,) he will not know us.

8. [After his fight [with Marie]] I left.

9. (After he fought [with Marie]) I left.

Exercise 2

1. I will come [to the party] (no matter what you say.)

2. I will be happy (no matter what present you give me.)

3. (However sick you are,) you still must work.

4. (Whenever he arrives,) I can pick him up.

5. I finished my work (in order that I might rest briefly.)

6. (Whatever you do (while you are depressed,)) I will still care [for you.]

Lesson 17

1. [In order to be prepared [for class]] I reread my notes.

2. [In order for him to be elected president,] I must write this speech.

3. (In order that I might be wealthy,) I invested [in a roulette wheel.]

4. (While I was studying [in order to pass the test,]) I was not working.

5. [To get the tickets,] I stood [in line] [for a long time.]

6. (After Bob worked so hard [to pass the test]) I talked [to him] [about his fear [of failure.]]

Lesson 18

1. Bob ate wisely, but he gained weight.

2. Bob and Ted did the work [without other help.]

3. He was fired, for he stole some things [from his company.]

4. He went [to the grocery store] [for milk.]

5. [In order for him to be elected [without a runoff]] he must get a large majority [of the urban vote.]

6. I quit, so I am poor.

7. I quit (so I could have more free time.)

8. He was fired (because he stole [from his company]) and (because he was insubordinate.)

9. I talked [to Hal and Tim] [about their opportunities [for promotion.]]

Lesson 19

1. Bob complained regularly, but he would not work.
   - S: Bob / VI: complained / CC: but / S: he / would not / VI: work

2. (Although Susan works hard,) she makes little money.
   - VMClɑ: Although / S: Susan / VI: works / hard / S: she / VT: makes / little / DO: money

3. I lost my job. However, Bob was hired.
   - S: I / VT: lost / my / DO: job / CA: However / S: Bob / was / Vtp: hired

4. I lost my job. Bob was hired, though.
   - S: I / VT: lost / my / DO: job / S: Bob / was / Vtp: hired / CA: though

5. I lost my job. (In contrast,) Bob was hired.
   - S: I / VT: lost / my / DO: job / op: In / contrast / S: Bob / was / Vtp: hired

6. I lost my wallet; consequently, I have no money.
   - S: I / VT: lost / my / DO: wallet / CA: consequently / S: I / VT: have / no / DO: money

Lesson 20

1. The man said (that I was lying.)
   - The / S: man / VT: said / DO NCl: that / S: I / was / VI: lying

2. That man lied.
   - That / S: man / VT: lied

3. That is true.
   - S: That / Vlw: is / PA: true

4. (So that we would be ready,) I thought (that we should study.)
   - VMCl: So that / S: we / Vlw: would / be / PA: ready / S: I / VT: thought / DO NCl: that / S: we / should / VT: study

5. I know that.
   - S: I / VT: know / DO: that

6. I think (that that hat looks awful.)
   - S: I / VT: think / DO NCl: that / that / S: hat / Vlw: looks / PA: awful

7 I understand (he lost his job [at the mall.])
   - S: I / VT: understand / that: / S: he / VT: lost / his / DO: job / op: at / the / op: mall

8. The truth is (that I am happy.)
   - The / S: truth / Vlw: is / PA NCl: that / S: I / Vlw: am / PA: happy

148   English Syntax

Lesson 21

Exercise 1

1. It is true (that Harold won the race.)

2. (That we were sick) was unfortunate.

3. It is regrettable (that you made that mistake.)

4. (That he missed the bus) is possible.

5. It is certain (that the party will be formal.)

6. I know (that it is true (that Harold won the race.))

7. (That he poisoned the weeds yesterday) is true.

8. It is doubtful (the senate will pass the bill now.)

9. He knows (that I am his friend.)

10. It is shameful (that we have a rat [in our barn.])

Exercise 2

1. He said (that he knew (that you would quit.))

2. He must have forgotten (that you worked [at that shoe store] [for thirty years.])

3. It is certain (that he was sick.)

4. I doubt (that it is certain (that he was sick.))

5. The ring is beautiful, but it does not appeal [to me.]

6. It is the one [with the large diamond.]

7. It is truly beautiful.

8. (That it is truly beautiful) is true.

9. It is true (that it is truly beautiful.)

Lesson 22

1. I know (who won.)

2. I know (what you ate.)

3. I know (why you cried.)

4. The teacher thought (that you cried.)

5. The man knows (what he likes.)

6. The elephant remembered (who hurt him.)

7. The plumber knew (where he could find the pipes.)

8. The telephone company knew (who was making the crank calls.)

9. He forgot (which key opened the door.)

10. He understood (how brave you were.)

Lesson 23

1. (Whoever finishes first) leaves first.
2. I like (whatever you like.)
3. I like (whatever happens.)
4. I like (what happened.)
5. (Whenever we should go) has not been decided.
6. (Whosever car that is) should be happy.
7. I know (that (whatever he says) is true.)

Lesson 24

1 I do not understand (whether or not Marie will be living alone.)
2. He doesn't know (if he will go [to the play] or not.)
3. He may not have known (whether he would support the group or fight [against them.])
4. I cannot remember (whether he likes pasta or not.)

Lesson 25

1. I like to wash my dog.

2. I would like for you to wash my dog.

3. I know that he washed the dog.

4. When he tried to remove the burr, the dog whined.

5. He started to get personal, and they objected to his behavior.

6. They went to town to buy some milk for the children, for they hate for them to be thirsty.

Lesson 26

1. It is smart to leave the party early.

2. To be a hero is not very difficult if you are brave and talented.

3. To be early for my appointments, I must start to get ready quite soon.

4. It is possible for me to arrive somewhere early.

5. I wanted to buy a car, so I priced one, but it was too expensive.

6. It is unlikely that I will buy it now.

Lesson 27

Exercise 1

1. I expect him to forget her.
2. I told Margie to buy the hat.
3. I went to town to buy the hat.
4. I hate for her to buy that outlandish hat.
5. I asked him to be quiet about his discovery until he got his patent.
6. When he agreed to remain quiet, I was glad.

Exercise 2

1. I hate to stop now.
2. I wanted to give Bob a tie.
3. I decided to buy a car.
4. I expect you to understand.
5. I saw him hit the car.
6. I saw that he hit the car.
7. I had him paint my house.
8. I want her to write you a note.
9. I asked her something.
10. I guess the man quit.
11. I wanted him to quit.
12. I watched him quit.

Exercise 3

1. That man hates to quit early.
2. I know (that he saw her fall into the river.)
3. This man thinks (you are rich.)
4. [From a distance] I could hear him sing but I could not hear his lyrics.
5. (When we were closing,) I saw him kiss her.
6. I guess (you know (which car will win the race.))
7. It was dangerous [for you to say (that Fred hated to be married to Marie.)]
8. (Whoever hates to live alone) should not marry.
9. I forgot (why he wanted to hear me read.)
10. [For you to want to own a dog in the dorm] was stupid.

Lesson 28

Exercise 1

1. I forgot [how to tune my car.]
2. I remember [which marks to use.]
3. I know [how fast to drive on my road.]
4. I don't know [where to go tonight.]
5. I forget [what to call the baby.]
6. I don't know [whose to borrow.]
7. The boy does not know [what to give his sister for her birthday.]
8. Marie knew [why to study for the test.]

Exercise 2

1. I know what she told Mary.
2. She knew what information to give Mary.
3. I hope that he remembers what to do when he goes into the game.
4. I heard what Martha said to Mary about what to feed the baby.
5. I heard the baby cry, but I did not know what to do to stop her.
6. I hope that she remembers to leave me instructions about what I should feed the baby.
7. I want Bill to tell me what to say to George when he arrives from work.

Lesson 29

1. I like floating down the river.
2. Being a king is not easy.
3. I want them to like writing poems.
4. Saying that I was a renegade was unwise.
5. In order for me to finish doing my chores by breakfast, I must arise at dawn.
6. They talked about telling us to quit early.
7. Starting to eat before we get to the table is rude.

Lesson 30

Exercise 1

1. I quit talking in class.

2. He was talking about dropping English.

3. His task is painting the ceiling.

4. Painting the ceiling blue should be easy.

5. He is crying.

6. Bob has been writing letters to Susan.

7. He likes my singing.

8. Being clean is important.

9. I saw him leave.

10. Dancing is interesting.

Exercise 2

1. I know why he hates washing that dog.

2. Saying that I was a liar was stupid.

3. I know who hates polishing the floor.

4. The people knew who liked living near the freeway.

5. The people preferred a more remote location and continued looking.

6. He tried cooking.

7. He began to like trying to cook.

8. He left without explaining why he did not want us to quit singing our song.

9. I heard him saying that he had watched us win the contest.

Lesson 31

1. The boy (who borrowed my bike) will return it later.

2. The flag (which waved [above my school]) disappeared yesterday.

3. Bob bought the bike (that I wanted.)

4. The boy (whom you invited [to the party]) came later.

5. He came late [to the party (which I gave.)]

6. A man (who is a doctor) lives [in the apartment (which my father bought.)]

7. The tree (that you climbed) is tall.

8. A girl (who is tall) may play basketball.

Lesson 32

1. The people (whom you invited) came [to the party.]

2. He knows the mechanic (whom you hired.)

3. The park ([at which] you played) was attractive.

4. The lot (which you parked [in]) has an attendant.

5. The lifeguard (whom you know) waved [to us.]

6. The people (who lived here [during the winter]) left

   a message (which we must find.)

Lesson 33

Exercise 1

1. The place (where we entered) was open today [for some reason.]

2. The day (when I hit the long double) was the day (when I became a hitter.)

3. The reason (why he left) is unclear.

4. The moment (at which he arose) was important.

5. The boy (who sat [on the table]) broke its leg.

6. Tom knows the day (when the store gets the watermelons.)

7. I know the spot (where the wreck occurred.)

Exercise 2

1. The boy (who lives [near the pond]) skates there [during the winter.]

2. The goats (which you sold) ran away.

3. The carpenter (whose tools are sharp) can do good work.

4. Carolyn likes the café (where they serve the delicious shrimp.)

5. A man (whom I know) won the contest [during the festival.]

6. The car (which I wrecked) is a pile [of junk] now.

7. Lettuce is a vegetable (which I like.)

8. I like the driver (whose car finished the race first.)

Lesson 34

Exercise 1

1. Margie, (who lives across the street) plays the drums [after midnight.]

2. Ft. Worth, (where the west begins,) is a large city now.

3. The Sabine river, (which flows from the North,) is the Eastern boundary [of Texas.]

4. My son, (who likes mysteries,) loves your book.

Exercise 2

1. Mary Casper, who had been our president, talked yesterday at our meeting

2. The tree that he cut was sick.

3. The time when he came was inappropriate.

4. He hit Carolyn Tobin, who was innocent.

5. Mom, who loves animals, hated my cute, little snake.

Lesson 35

1. We scared the deer (which were eating the vegetables (that we had planted in the spring))

2. I saw the man (who had the car (which had the bumper (which had the sticker (which had the letters (that glowed.)))))

3. The plumber (that the mechanic (who fixed our car) recommended) fixed our pipes.

4. The cornerback tackled the end (who had received the pass (which the quarterback threw.))

Lesson 36

1. The people (who are swimming in the swift water) must be careful.

2. The dog {barking at the postman} is a nuisance.

3. The people {eating the popcorn so loud} are sitting behind me.

4. I talked to the men {being given the award} about their honor.

5. The dog {being a nuisance} is my dog.

6. The man {giving the children the balloons} is George Ogilvie.

7. The people (who have been staying here) may be leaving soon.

8. I want one of the pies {cooling on the top shelf of the pie safe.}

Lesson 37

Exercise 1

2a. The trees (which were chopped [by the lumberjacks] yesterday) have been towed away.

2b. The trees {chopped [by the lumberjacks] yesterday} have been towed away.

3a. Sylvia admired the poems (which were written [by her friend.])

3b. Sylvia admired the poems {written [by her friend.]}

4a. Fred hated the man (who was elected president.)

4b. Fred hated the man {elected president.}

5a. The man (who was given the award) smiled broadly.

5b. The man {given the award} smiled broadly.

Exercise 2

1. The people packed into the stadium had watched a great game.

2. I think that the people who were sent the invitation enclosed in the blue envelopes came to the party.

3. The pies eaten by the contestant were tasteless.

4. The trees cut by Bill were used for posts.

5. The student elected cheerleader by the judges chosen by the students were seniors.

Lesson 38

1. We elected Tim captain.

2. I talked to Hiram Golightly, the custodian, about the bad light.

3. Boston, sometimes called Bean town, is the home of the Red Sox.

4. Bill Smith, whose friend, George Brown, owns a boat, often borrows it.

5. I consider Millicent Pembroke, our guide, a stuff shirt.

6. George Carson, who called himself the magnificent one, is a miserable failure.

7. Somebody gave George, our captain, the answers to the test.

8. I was replaced in the third inning by Bill Van Fleet, a wild lefthander who had lost his last three games.

9. My car, an old Olds, runs well on unleaded gas, a product sold everywhere.

10. He climbed the tree, a task easily accomplished.

Lesson 39

1. Helen has been here lately.
2. Joe is in the pool now.
3. The people in the pool are in the shade.
4. I am running away to my Uncle's house.
5. Chuck is in the dumps.
6. Gloria is on top of the world.
7. The people swimming in the deep water are in trouble.
8. Harry Bartlett, my doctor in Austin, is an osteopath.

Lesson 40

1. I know the car that you should give me.
2. I know the car for you to give me. {the car}
3. The girl that we should choose captain is Michelle.
4. The girl for us to choose captain is Michelle.
5. The people who will be given the prize are happy.
6. The people to be given the prize are happy.
7. The race for us to win is the 10K.
8. The room for us to work in is the kitchen.
9. The character for me to be is Hamlet.

Lesson 41

1. I am scared (that Bo will arrive early.)
2. He is confident (that I can win.)
3. It is doubtful (that I can win.)
4. He is doubtful (that I can win.)
5. I am certain (that I will win.)
6. I am certain to win.
7. It is certain (that I will win.)
8. I know (that I will win.)

Lesson 42

1. Bob is so tired (that he has curled up [on the floor.])
2. I hope (that he is not so angry (that he will hit me.)
3. I am so happy (that I think (that I will cry.)
4. He hit me, so I cried.
5. I saved money (so that I could go [to Boston.])
6. I guess (that I am so mistreated (that I should quit.))

Lesson 43

1. I run as fast (as Bill does. run fast)
2. He is not so fast (as Bill. is fast)
3. I was more disturbed (than I have been disturbed lately.)
4. I do not start as quickly (as Fred does start quickly.)
5. He plays so hard (that he grows tired early.)
6. Bob is less considerate (than Marie is. considerate.)

Lesson 44

1. He came yesterday.
2. He left today.
3. He will return the day (that we paint the barn.)
4. I will finish college next semester.
5. He will leave the second (that he finishes.)
6. The day (that he arrived) was beautiful.
7. He walks that way intentionally.
8. The man will complete the task the month [after the election.]
9. I forgot [to buy a newspaper] this morning.
10. The morning (when it snowed) I was [in New York.]
11. The way (that you walk) is silly.
12. You walk [in a silly way.]

Lesson 45

1. He watched the game, staring intently at every play.

2. The people were dancing enthusiastically, their feet beating wildly in the red dust.

3. They came to the party with their jeans tucked in their outlandish boots.

4. I attended college, hoping that I would have enough money to finish.

5. He came to the party, wearing rings in his nose, his hair dyed indigo.

6. Whoever wants to know what Bob wants must follow him daily, hanging on his every word.

7 His boots unshined, his hair streaming wildly, his hand holding his hat high above his head, he rode into the ballroom, still smiling his silly way.

Lesson 46

1. I saw him beaten by the gang.

2. I heard the music played by him.

2. I heard the music played by him.

3. I heard it played by him.

4. I saw him being beaten by the gang.

5. I watched the car be wrecked.

Lesson 47

1. He is going to be given the award.

2. He used to want to work to make money.

3. Bob has to stop (what he has been saying.)

4. I think he is going to be good [at marking sentences.]

5. Bob has to be working late tonight.

6. Bill will have to complete the book.

Lesson 48

1. I went to see the movie.

2. I quit (in order that I might stay [with my family.)

3. To win, Bob would cheat.

4. I want to see the movie.

3. I hate for him to see the movie.

4. I know (what I should see.)

5. I know what to see.

6. I saw him go [into the movie]]

7. I know the movie (which you should see.)

8. I know the movie [for you to see. {the movie}]

9. I told him to go [to the movie.]]

10. I stopped [in order to rest.]

11. He is sure to attend the lecture.

12. He is sure (that he will attend the lecture.)

166   English Syntax

Lesson 49

1. (When he came here,) I was sure (that he would wear that tacky hat (that he likes.))

2. He said (that he would wear (whatever he liked.))

2. I heard that, but I don't believe (that (what he said) was true.)

3. That story has been told [about him] before.

4. I am so confident [about his {not saying that}] (that I will bet [on it.])

5. (Provided that he avoids {wearing that hat}) I think the people (that know him) will be sure (that he has a good time.))

6. I don't know [what to say [about Bob's {running so fast (that he lost his shoes.)}

7. That tree (that he climbed) was so tall (that we could not see him [in the high branches.])

8. That is not good (because {being so high} is dangerous.)

Lesson 50

1. I learned when to be quiet.

2. I stopped work (when the whistle blew.)

3. (No matter where I work,) I can hear the whistle.

4. The reason (why I quit) was (that I was paid poorly.)

5. I learned (where the treasure maps were hid.)

6. The house (where he lived) was haunted.

7. I don't know (why he quit.)

8. The day (when I was born) was cold.

9. I know when to quit.

10. (When Bob arrived at the ranch) the horses had been stolen.

11. I know how to ride.

12. I know (how angry he is.)

13. (No matter how angry he is), he must control his temper.

Lesson 51

1. I think (he knows [whose car to borrow.])

2. The man (whose car you borrowed) is calling the police.

3. (No matter whose secrets you told,) that is wrong.

4. He knows (whose secrets are most important.)

5. I remember (which pie you ate.)

6. And you know (which I like.)

7. The house (which he bought) was haunted.

8. The note (which he printed) was libelous.

8. The house (which he lived [in]) was haunted.

9. The house (which he lived in) was ugly.

9. The house ([in which] he lived) was haunted.

10. The house (where he lived) was haunted.

11. What did he say?

12. What lesson did you learn?

13. Bess will fire him (no matter what he says.)

14. I don't know [what to give her.]

Appendix 2

Answers to Practices

Practice 1

Exercise 1

1. The ice storm had been predicted [by some astute meteorologists.]

2. The man [on Channel 10] has been calling it a disaster.

3. Some people have fallen [because of the slickness [of the steps.]]

4. The steps [below the library] should be considered dangerous [during an ice storm.]

5. Bob Larsen may have been the best weather forecaster [before his dismissal [for drunkenness.]]

6. The station did pay him his severance pay willingly.

7. He should be angry [about their treatment [of him.]]

8. [Before the show] he had been drinking [for several hours [at a neighborhood bar] [with his friends.]]

9. He was selected as chief meteorologist [in 1994.]

10. He was given a plaque [at the time] [in addition to a raise.]

11. Bob may have been paid well [for his success [at weather prediction.]]

12. He might be getting a new job soon.

13. He could become a bartender.

Exercise 2

1. I have been feeling sorry for Fred because of his illness.

2. I gave the candy to Fred in the cafeteria before lunch.

3. His illness should not be considered trivial.

4. Mine should not have been serious.

5. I have always been a healthy person.

6. He was not given the candy by a friend.

7. The candy was given him by an enemy.

8. I am the purveyor of the candy.

9. He does not consider me guilty.

10. I have been called a poisoner by his true friends.

11. I was just telling George the story about Fred today.

12. George is blaming me for Fred's illness.

13. They consider my explanations inadequate.

Exercise 3

1. He has been fishing [in the lake] [since noon.]
2. Some expert fishermen consider him a good fishermen.
3. He can cast a fly [into a small spot] excellently.
4. Fish have been caught [by him] [in unlikely places.]
5. The fish become wary [in the late afternoon] [because of the long shadows.]
6. I was given a fish yesterday [by my neighbor.]
7. I may remain happy [with this fish]
8. I am not considered a good fishermen [by Jimmy.]
9. He could have been good [at his job.]
10. He is considered lucky [by many] [of his friends.]
11. He may have been cheating [in the bass contest.]

Practice 2

Exercise 1

1. The anxious parents had been observing the children attentively.

2. Some people might consider them overprotective.

3. However, they should give the children their full attention.

4. They probably have been parents [for years,] and they may be aware [of some dangers.]

5. Bears have been seen nearby, and they are considered dangerous. sometimes.

6. Otherwise, parents have been worrying [without proper cause.]

7. We were sent letters [by the park service,] but I remain confident [of our safety.]

8. Dogs and cats are being kept inside [by some pet owners.]

9. Dogs and bears do not become friends easily, so our dogs must be protected.

10. The neighborhood dog is called Leo or Rocky Road, for he has two owners.

11. We called him Ugly Puppy [at first.]

12. The house should be repainted [before your party.]

13. They might have been lying [about the bears.]

Exercise 2

1. Some people are unhappy (when they are given Romaine lettuce.)

2. (Although I have been reading a novel,) I have not finished it yet.

3. Bill will be returning soon [from his vacation] (even though he has not been missed.)

4. [Because of his laziness,] we do not complete our work promptly.

5. (Because he is exceedingly lazy,) we are usually quite late [with our assignments.]

6. Our boss gave him a warning [about his work habits] (before he left [for his vacation.])

7. [Before his return] we should plan a practical joke (so that he will know [about our affection [for him.]])

8. (If you return late,) Tom may be angry (when you arrive.)

9. [Despite your anger,] your mother probably loves you.

10. [In case of fire,] you should evacuate the building (even if you consider yourself safe.)

Exercise 3

1. Jim has been sending Milly messages about his concern [for her welfare.]

2. (When she gets the messages [from him,]) she feels happy, but no message is sent [to him] [in return] for she is shy.

3. [In order for him to be her beau,] he must be encouraged (because he is considered shy, too.)

4. [Because of her interest [in him]] she talks [to her friend] [to get advice.]

5. Her friend is a woman [with impeccable credentials [in matters [of love]] (since she has had four husbands.)

6. (While talking [to her friend,]) she discovers the truth [about her affection [for Jim.]]

7. Therefore, she chooses him as her date [for the first dance [of the season.]]

8. She has never attended a dance [before this,] yet she has seen them and has heard [about them] [from her friend.]

9. He might be considered a poor catch [by many people,] but he is considered wonderful [by Milly.]

10. [For her to be truly happy,] she must wear a beautiful gown [to the dance.]

11. He may dance the strange way [of his people.]

12. He will probably take her home two minutes [after the dance] (in order that he might watch the Cowboy's game [at the bar.])

Exercise 4

1. The tree [on the corner] should be removed [to keep the other trees healthy.]

2. (Because George will be working late,) he will probably be late.

3. (Although I call George a loser sometimes,) he is considered successful [by most [of his friends.]]

4. [In order for us to learn [about George]] we hired a detective.

5. (While I am working [in the garden]) I usually wear a hat or cap (in order that I might protect my face.)

6. Gardens are always sunny (if they are successful.)

7. I have not been a good gardener, for I have lost the war [with the grasshoppers, the brown spot, and the drouth.]

8. (No matter how smart you are,) you should attend class.

9. (Whatever you learn,) you will benefit [from it] (when you write.)

10. I will go [to see the movie] (no matter what you say.)

11. [In order to be given the award,] I must attend the ceremony (no matter what excuse I may have.)

Practice 3

Exercise 1

1. Now that I have given Bob whatever he wanted, I wish that I had seen how gluttonous he was.

2. Whichever book he buys will be the wrong one.

3. Whichever book he buys, he will pick the wrong one.

4. No matter where he hides, they will find him because they know where they must look in order to find culprits.

5. Whoever buys a good bicycle will have what he or she needs to arrive economically at his or her destination.

6. I wish that what he told you was the truth.

7. When he said that he knew what I knew, he was lying.

Exercise 2

1. I guess that you can't remember whether or not I told you what I would send you.

2. What I said was that I would give you another practice before you took the test.

3. I hope that you gave what I said your full attention.

4. When Bob was arrested after the party he was given a breathalyzer test in order to discover whether he had been drinking or not.

5. I suspect that the police thought that he was drunk because he was driving wildly.

6. Because of his arrest, he missed class and was given an F on his assignment.

7. No matter what he told the police, they still consider him guilty.

Exercise 3

1. I hope (that Bill will learn (where he should keep his valuables)

2. (If Fred is given a raise this week) he will be taking a vacation [to Tahiti] to rest [from his labors.]

3. (No matter what I am called,) I do not become angry (because I know (I will not be hurt [by (what someone calls me.)]))

4. [In order to be given the award,] I must remember (what the deadline [for entry] is.)

5. [Because of his misbehavior] my dog has been banished [to the yard] to consider his misdeeds [at his leisure.]

6. (However I feel today,) I must write (what I know [about the mystery [of life]])

7. (Although I know (whose bike was stolen [by Bill)]) I will not tell (what I know) (since I am afraid [of Bill.])

8. It is probable (that Hal had been a fascist,) but now I think (he has become a communist.)

9. My friend gave me a cold, and it has lasted a month.

10. (No matter how smart he is,) he cannot pass (unless he learns (how he should study.)

11. (When Bob was sent the letter,) he learned (when he would receive his award.)

12. (Whichever person wins the race) will be given (whatever reward that person wishes)

Exercise 4

1. I like giving my children presents.

2. I left without putting the cat out.

3. His removing the child from the well was heroic.

4. I regret leaving home.

5. Washing cars is his main skill.

6. His job is decorating houses.

7. He has been decorating houses for years.

8. Being called a wasp upsets Bob because he is an Irishman.

9. He came here after being fired in Baltimore.

10. Being a grammarian is a very good thing.

11. Riding a bicyle can be economical but tiring.

12. George talked about giving his son a bicycle.

13. Being given a bicycle by his father should please the boy.

14. Being a book thief is not good.

15. He left without saying what he would give his son for the birthday.

Exercise 5

1. I believe (that {taking tests} is easy (when I study.)

2. I know (that (what he wants) is {winning the lottery.})

3. (Although he thinks (that I forgot [about {loaning him the money,}) I remember that well.

4. (Whatever he says [about {returning the money}] is probably a lie.

5. (No matter where he is working,) he hates {being given poor tasks.}

6. I suspect {that} he has forgotten (which train he should take (when leaving Paris.)

7. I know (that {owning a home} can be expensive, but I will buy one (whatever it costs.)

8. {Being elected President} is not easy.

Exercise 6

1. I know that you believe that what I told you was nonsense.

2. It is possible that you forgot calling Bill an old goat, but I don't think that he will forget it soon.

3. No matter what you say to apologize, I bet he will still be angry about what you said.

4. Whoever talks to him should try to calm him down, for he has high blood pressure and it is dangerous for him to be angry.

5. Being called an old goat is not what made him mad though.

6. I heard him tell his wife that he is mad about your leaving his chain saw in the rain.

7. Although you can remember where you left it, you can't say that you did not know where to put it.

8. Marie and Bob have been having an argument about his watching her make a cake.

Practice 4

Exercise 1

1. Now I think that I know who stole the pie from the kitchen.

2. The pie he stole was probably still hot since I had just removed it from the oven.

3. I thought the place where I had stored it was safe, and I figured that I could see whatever happened there.

4. I had not seen my son going into the kitchen, yet I am sure that he must have taken the pie.

5. I do not want to call him a pie thief unless I have some evidence of his taking it.

6. He is so fond of pie that he probably would take it if he had known where I put it.

7. I wish that I had seen him come in last night so I could know when he came back.

8. The person who took it must have been here between seven and nine in order to have smelled it cooling.

9. It is likely that he came in later without making any noise.

10. But people stealing pies usually do not make a noise however hungry they are.

11. The pie taken from the shelf was a pie which my wife considered wonderful.

12. Pies I bake during the summer are pies treasured for their rarity.

Exercise 2

1. I guess that I should start keeping better records.

2. Whoever wants to write well should know what is happening in the world.

3. I am certain that people that save junk are people I would like.

4. He works so enthusiastically that he causes the other workers to be eager to work also.

5. While Bob was working for a little money in order to pay his bills, Dan was becoming more famous for gathering the news than Walter was.

6. I heard them say that they wanted to be as good as Dan and Walter were.

7. No matter where he worked, he did the dirty jobs because of his low self esteem, which was communicated in some fashion to the people employing him.

8. He was always in trouble because of his complaining about what he was given.

9. I am afraid to go to the place where I found the body.

10. A person given an award for writing a great book should be a person I would respect.

11. A place where you should visit on your vacation is a place at which good food is served.

1. Jim stood there, watching the crowd, his eyes constantly moving.

2. He has to be tired after watching the crowd intently so that he will miss nothing.

3. (Because he works hard,) I think that he is a more careful bodyguard than Bob was.

4. The man to hire for a bodyguard is one who works as carefully as Jim.

5. Jim has been chosen bodyguard of the year as a result of his extraordinarily careful work.

6. I am glad that he was hired to protect the mayor, my brother in law.

7. I am about to watch him work and I expect him to be as good as they have told me that he was.

8. The mayor wants me to learn how to do what Jim has been doing.

9. I think being a bodyguard as good as Jim is would be so difficult that I would fail.

10. The people attending the rally for the mayor stood in places where Jim could see them easily.

11. The place at which the rally was held was near the city hall.

Appendix 3

Word List

Pronouns

Personal Pronouns

I, me, you, he, him, she, her, it, we, us, they, them

Indefinite pronoun

someone, somebody, something, anyone, anybody, anything, no one, nobody, nothing, everybody, everything, everyone, another, others

Quantitative Pronouns

some, many, much, any, more, few, less, several, all, both, each, each one, each other, neither, either, most

Demonstrative Pronouns

this, that, these, those

Possessive Pronouns

mine, yours, his, her, its, ours, theirs

Adjectivals

Demonstrative Adjectives

this, that, these, those

Possessive Adjectives

my, your, his, her, its, our, their

Verbs

Linking Verbs

be, become, remain, appear, seem, feel, get, turn, act, grow

Verbs frequently followed by Indirect Objects and Direct Objects

give, hand, throw, toss, mail, send, make, call

Verbs frequently followed by Retained Objects

be given, be handed, be thrown, be tossed, be mailed, be sent, be made, be called

Verbs frequently followed by Direct Objects and Object Complements

pick, select, elect, choose, pick, paint, name, make, call

Verbs frequently followed by Retained Object Complements

be picked, be selected, be chosen, be elected, be painted, be named, be made, be called

Verbs frequently followed by infinitive phrases with structure words _for_ and _to_

hate, like, love, intend, prefer

Verbs frequently followed by infinitive phrases without structure words

want, expect, require, allow

Verbs frequently followed by indirect object and infinitive phrases

ask, tell, beg, promise, advise, order, urge, dare

Verbs frequently followed by infinitive phrases without structure words _for_ and _to_

see, hear, feel, watch, listen to, smell, let, help, make, have

Verbs followed by past participle phrase as nominal

see, hear, feel, watch, listen to, smell

Auxiliary Verbs and Modals

be, have, do, may, might, can, could, shall, should, will, would, must

Compound Auxiliary Verbs

be going to, be to, be about to, be fixing to, have to, used to, ought to

Adverbials

Conjunctive Adverbs

afterwards, also, concurrently, consequently, hence, henceforth, hereafter, however, later, meantime, meanwhile, moreover, nevertheless, next, nonetheless, once, otherwise, then, thereafter, therefore, though, thus, too

Single Word Adverbs

above, accordingly, again, again and again, ahead, alone, already, also, always, annually, anyhow, anyway, anyways, anywhere, around, away, below, besides, biweekly, candidly, continually, daily, doubtless, early, endlessly, fittingly, forth, forward, frankly, frequently, honestly, however, infrequently, instead, instead, late, later, maybe, momentarily, monthly, more, never, next, now, occasionally, often, once, out, overhead, perhaps, possibly, quarterly, rarely, seldom, semiweekly, so far, sometimes, somewhere, soon, still, surely, then, together, up, weekly, yearly, yesterday, yet

Prepositional Phrases like Conjunctive Adverbs

after this, as a result, as a result of this, as a substitute, as an alternative, at this time, because of this, despite that, despite this, for a week, for that reason, from this time, in a way that accords with that, in accordance, in accordance with that, in addition, in addition to that, in conclusion, in contrast, in contrast to that, in lieu of that, in place of that, in spite of that, in summary, in summation, in that case, in that event, in time, instead of that, no doubt, of course, on occasions, on the other hand, since that time, since then, under those circumstances, within the hour

Connectives

Coordinating Conjunction

for, so, and, but, yet, or, nor

Introducers of Clause Modifying Verbs, type 1

after, although, as, because, before, if, once, provided, providing, since, so, supposing, that, though, unless, until, when, where, whereas, while

Introducers of Clause Modifying Verbs, type 1, Compounds

along with the fact that, as a result of the fact that, as often as, as if, as soon as, as soon as it happened that, as though, at the place that, at the time that, because of the fact that, despite the fact that, due to the fact that, during the time that, in addition to the fact that, in case, in case that, in contrast to the fact that, in hopes that, in order that, in spite of the fact that, owing to the fact that, plus the fact that, even though, every time that, in the event, in the event that, now that, provided that, providing that, since the time that, so that, supposing that, with the fact that, within the period of time that

Introducers of Clause Modifying Verbs, type 2

whatever, whichever, whoever, whomever, whosoever, wherever, whenever, however, no matter what, no matter whom, no matter who, no matter which, no matter whose, no matter how, no matter when, no matter why, no matter how often, no matter how long

Introducers of Noun Clauses, type 1

no function in clause

that

Introducers of Noun Clauses, type 2

as nominals

who, whom, which, what, whose

as adjectivals

whose, which, what, how

as adverbials

how, where, when, why

Introducers of Noun Clauses, type 3

as nominals

whoever, whatever, whichever, whatever, whosoever, whatsoever

as adjectivals

whosoever, whichever, whatever, however

as adverbials

wherever, whenever, however

Introducers of Noun Clauses, type 4

no function in clause

if ____or not, whether or not, whether____ or not

Introducers of Noun-Modifying Clauses *(Also called relative clauses and adjectival clauses)*

as nominals

who, whom, which

as adjectivals

whose

as adverbials

where, when, why

Single Word Prepositions

aboard, about, above, across, after, against, along, along with, amid, among, around, at, at, barring, before, behind, below, beneath, beside, besides, between, beyond, by, concerning, despite, down, during, except, excepting, for, from, in, inside, instead, into, like, near, of, off, on, outside, over, past, plus, regarding, respecting, save, saving only, through, throughout, till, to, together with, toward, towards, until, up, upon, with, within, without

Compound Prepositions

à la, as a result of, aside from, because of, by dint of, by means of, by the use of, by way of, contrary to, due to, for the sake of, in addition to, in advance of, in case of, in conjunction with, in consideration of, in contrast to, in hope of, in hopes of, in lieu of, in place of, in reference to, in regard to, in spite of, in the direction of, in the event of, in the fashion of, in the manner of, in the middle of, in the style of, instead of, on account of, on behalf of, out of, outside of, owing to, through the use of, with respect to, with the exception of